*The Life and World of*

# HENRY VIII

# The Life and World of
# HENRY VIII

❧ *Roberta Strauss Feuerlicht* ❧

*Crowell-Collier Press*

Library of Congress Catalog Card Number: 72–114324

The Macmillan Company
866 Third Avenue
New York, New York 10022

Collier-Macmillan Canada Ltd., Toronto, Ontario

Printed in the United States of America

FIRST PRINTING

*For Herb*

*from the first and last of his wives*

I WISH all princes could pass some part of their lives in a private station, that they might know the wants of their subjects; and from suffering themselves, learn to pity those who suffer. But, educated amid regal pomp, they have little feeling for the calamities of others.

They think it nothing that for a petty quarrel, or from vain ambition, fields, villages, and towns should be laid waste, a population consumed, and even nations subverted.

Who can see without groans, or hear without tears, the crowds of the aged and of infants rendered homeless and weeping about the churches: their property taken away by military violence, even of their friendly armies, and what is still more intolerable, destroyed and burnt before their eyes.

*Juan Luis Vives, Spanish
humanist and contemporary
of Henry VIII*

# ~ Contents

*The Life and World of*

❧ HENRY VIII ❧

EUROPE
*at the time of* HENRY VIII

0        Miles        300

SCOTLAND

IRELAND

N

YORKSHIRE

LINCOLNSHIRE

ENGLAND
Westminster
London

Southampton

Calais

ATLANTIC
OCEAN

ENGLISH CHANNEL

Boulogne

Tournai
Therouanne

Noyon

Paris

THE
HOLY
ROMAN
EMPIRE

FRANCE

VENICE

Pavia

Venice

C A S T I L E

Fuenterrabia
NAVARRE

ARAGON

S  P  A  I  N

Rome

MEDITERRANEAN SEA

palacio

# 1 ❧ The Founding Father

FOR THIRTY YEARS the houses of Lancaster and York had clashed over the throne of England. For thirty years rival nobles had played a bloody chess game, with England as the board, the people as pawns, and a real king as prize. No principle was involved; it was simply a ferocious power struggle. But in brawling for the crown, the contenders demeaned it. The people would not obey royal edicts, for today's monarch might be tomorrow's corpse. If the great nobles of the land would not respect the crown and the law, neither would the commoners. They ignored the senseless quarrel and tended to the business of survival.

History would later give the battles, beheadings, and blood-lettings that took place between 1455 and 1485 the pleasant name of the Wars of the Roses. But the roses had sharp thorns. To possess the throne, men slew their friends and their brothers. One king, Richard III, is believed to have had his boy nephews, twelve and ten years old, murdered because their claim to the crown was better than his.

It was this same Richard, of the house of York, who in August, 1485, rode forth to meet the challenge of the latest Lancaster, twenty-eight-year-old Henry Tudor. Henry's claim to the throne was flawed for it was through female descent and an illicit match, but he bolstered it considerably with an army of English loyalists and French mercenaries.

The forces of Richard and Henry met on August 22 near the village of Market Bosworth. Henry had some five thousand men; Richard raised twice that number. But the king knew that some of his nobles were disloyal and might well desert him on the field. The battle had scarcely begun when he made a heroic but desperate decision to chance all on one brilliant stroke. He would slay Henry Tudor in hand-to-hand combat and secure his throne with his own axe.

With less than one hundred men, Richard galloped across the field to where Henry sat on horseback. A gold coronet glinted on Richard's steel helmet, so everyone would know who was king of England.

Richard of York tried to slash his way through Henry's guard, but he fell beneath the flailing axes and swords. The king was dead. The coronet that toppled from his battered and bloodied helmet was found in a hawthorn bush and raised to the brow of Henry Tudor.

Chance had placed a new line on the throne of England, but no one knew how long it might survive. In the past quarter of a century, three men and a boy had been king of England; only one had died a natural death. In theory the crown was hereditary, but it had not passed safely from father to son in Henry's lifetime.

In the closing decades of the fifteenth century, after thirty years of civil war, which followed more than one hundred years of war with France, England was governed neither by king nor Parliament but by anarchy and chaos. There was little central authority; instead, mighty nobles ruled vast areas with private armies. In the absence of order, English trade and commerce lagged behind that of other nations. The crown itself was in debt, and some of the crown jewels had been pawned. Because the king of England had no power at home, he had none abroad and other monarchs sought neither his advice nor his alliance.

Henry Tudor had not spent his life training to be a statesman but as an exile living on the crumbs of foreign courts. Yet he knew what he wanted, and because the people wanted it too, he was to become one of England's greatest kings.

Within three months after he was crowned Henry VII in Westminster Abbey, he tried to unite the warring houses of Lancaster and York by marrying Elizabeth, the daughter and sister of Yorkist kings. She was the niece of Richard III; the two slain youths were her brothers.

If Elizabeth was happy to love a Lancaster and let him rule, other Yorkists were not. Henry took the precaution of imprisoning the chief Yorkist heir, the ten-year-old earl of Warwick. But there were still two major Yorkist uprisings, with lowborn youths posing as pretenders to the throne. Henry crushed both rebellions and put the first pretender to work in the palace kitchen. The second had been a much more serious threat, and Henry had him executed, along with the real earl.

Young Warwick was an exception, however, for political executions were rare in Henry's reign. When the people rose in rebellion, Henry punished them by imposing high fines. The people liked a good execution but hated a hard tax, so they grew less rebellious, though not before Henry became the richest king England had ever known.

In gathering his fortune, Henry could be both shrewd and devious. The only time he went to war, Parliament voted him funds to do battle with the ancient enemy, France. He sailed to France with a large army but stayed only long enough to frighten the French king into buying peace. Then Henry sailed for home, pocketing both the parliamentary grant and the French bribe. It was not heroic but it was good finance and good sense, since the English would not have won anyway.

Henry VII came to power in an age of transition. It was the twilight of the Middle Ages and the dawn of the Renaissance. During Henry's reign, a Genoese mapmaker named Bartholomew Columbus came to court. Bartholomew had a brother named Christopher who thought he could reach the exotic lands of the East by sailing west across the great ocean. Would Henry finance such a voyage?

While Henry was making up his mind, Christopher Columbus set sail in the *Santa María*. Thus America was sighted under the flag of Ferdinand and Isabella of Spain rather than Henry VII of England. The English king was more receptive to the next explorer, and John Cabot sailed to North America under the flag of England.

At the same time the New World was being discovered, the Old World was rediscovering itself. Strong national states were emerging in western Europe, wed to the destiny of a single ruler or dynasty. The expansion of commerce created a new class—the middle class—whose members were neither high nor low, but powerful and mobile because they had money. The old nobility held the sword, but the middle class held the purse.

Because the nobility had brought little but war and crisis to England, Henry favored the middle class, for they, like he, were self-made men. Other kings had chosen only nobles for their council; Henry chose men of undistinguished birth but great ability. As a result Henry's advisers were not only more able but more loyal. Having been raised to high position by the king, they knew he could level them as well.

The whole thrust of Henry's reign was to centralize power in the person of the king and to curb the power of the nobles. He forced them to swear not to maintain private armies and he used the courts to bring them to heel. England had the forms of justice but not the substance, because the nobles considered themselves above the law. Henry therefore turned his council into a court that met at Westminster Palace, in a room that had stars depicted on the ceiling and was known as the Star Chamber. In the Court of Star Chamber, there was no jury to be bribed, and the judges could not be intimidated. Because it lacked the safeguards of the regular courts, the Star Chamber would eventually become an instrument of tyranny. But in the time of Henry VII it was the only court in England where a poor man could bring suit against a rich lord and win.

By the end of the fifteenth century, after nearly fifteen years of Henry's rule, the ambassador from Venice could report: "The kingdom of England has never for many years been so obedient to its sovereign as it is at present to his Majesty the king."

The people were content. They wanted peace, justice, and

stability, which Henry gave them. They needed strong central authority, and Henry provided it. Fortunes were being made from wool and cloth, and London was growing large and prosperous. New schools were being founded, and books were being printed and read. New ideas were carried from Italy by travelers and diplomats, and foreign scholars, artists, and craftsmen were welcomed at court by the cosmopolitan king.

What the English wanted most of all, Henry also gave them. They wanted an end to the quarrel over the throne, and Henry not only made it strong and stable, but he produced sons to inherit it.

Four of the seven children born to Henry Tudor and Elizabeth of York survived infancy, including two sons, Arthur and Henry. When Henry was born on June 28, 1491, the heir to the throne was his older brother, Arthur. Unlike Arthur, who was sickly, Henry was a healthy little boy whose face mirrored the features of the future king, with wide jowls, a tight Cupid's bow mouth, and skeptical eyes peering beneath swollen lids.

Young Henry's education was probably supervised by his learned grandmother, Margaret Beaufort, and his tutors included John Skelton, the poet laureate of England. Henry had a quick and active mind. He learned to speak Latin and French fluently and was a good student of theology and mathematics. He was fond of sport and music all of his life, and even as a youngster he had his own band of minstrels to play for him. He himself played the organ, the lute, and the harpsichord, and he wrote both poetry and music.

At the turn of the century, the wandering Dutch philosopher, Desiderius Erasmus, visited England, and Thomas More, then a bright young lawyer and scholar, took him to visit the royal children.

"Thomas More came to see me," wrote Erasmus, "and took me out with him for a walk as far as the next village, where all the king's children, except Prince Arthur, who was then the eldest son, were being educated. When we came into the hall, the attendants . . . were all assembled. In the midst stood Prince Henry, then nine years old, and having already something of royalty in his demeanor, in which there was a certain dignity combined with singular courtesy. . . .

"After paying his respects to the boy Henry . . . [More] presented him with some writing. For my part, not having expected anything of the sort, I had nothing to offer, but promised that, on another occasion, I would in some way declare my duty toward him. Meantime, I was angry with More for not having warned me, especially as the boy sent me a little note, while we were at dinner, to challenge something from my pen."

While young Henry was begging poems from Erasmus and playing and learning with his two sisters in the English country-side, his older brother Arthur had undertaken the sterner duties of heir to the throne. As prince of Wales he was living on the bleak Welsh border, and as his father's heir he was Henry VII's prize pawn in Europe's fascinating marriage game.

Royal marriages were made not in Heaven but in the councils of Europe. Personal feelings were not an issue, and many royal children were betrothed several times until the match was politically just right. A good marriage could strengthen a dynasty, add territory to a kingdom, settle a war, win a strong ally, or bring a fortune in dowry.

Henry VII arranged his children's marriages skillfully. He married his older daughter Margaret to King James IV of Scotland, which was then an independent and hostile kingdom on England's northern border. By making the Scottish king his son-in-law, Henry hoped to gentle England's traditional enemy and free his border from harassment.

The king considered betrothing both Henry and his sister Mary to the grandchildren of Maximilian, the Holy Roman Emperor, but for Arthur, his heir, Henry sought a very special bride. When the boy was less than two years old, Henry proposed a match between his son and Catalina, the youngest daughter of King Ferdinand and Queen Isabella of Spain. Catalina, nine months older than Arthur, was not yet three.

Both Henry VII and Ferdinand had much to gain from a marriage alliance. Ferdinand and Isabella saw in Henry an ally against their perpetual enemy, France. Henry saw Catalina's substantial dowry, but even more desirable was the pure royal blood she would give to his descendants. Henry could not forget that he was an adventurer who, using a tainted claim, had seized the throne by force. Catalina was the child of one of the oldest and most powerful royal families in Europe. Through her mother, she was directly and legitimately descended from Henry's ancestor, John of Gaunt, duke of Lancaster. Her marriage to Henry's son would secure the claim of the dynasty he had set upon the throne.

The marriage was arranged after many years of haggling

and negotiation. In August, 1501, the fifteen-year-old princess of Aragon sailed from Spain to England to become Arthur's wife. She was a pretty girl, with an oval face and long, reddish-brown hair.

Catalina, now called Catherine, was conducted into London by her future brother-in-law, Henry, a husky boy of ten. When she and Arthur were wed on November 14, 1501, it was Prince Henry, dressed in white velvet, who led the bride up the aisle.

The festivities over, Arthur had to return to his duties on the Welsh border, and his bride went with him. After four months, both fell ill. Arthur, who was frail and tubercular, died on April 2, 1502. At the age of sixteen, Catherine of Aragon was a widow.

With Arthur's death, the first question that occurred to the Spanish ambassador was whether Catherine might be pregnant. She could at least be queen-mother, if not queen, and Spain would get something out of its investment. But Catherine was not pregnant, so another question occurred to him. Had the marriage ever been consummated?

Because the teen-aged bride and groom were the children of monarchs, dynasties and fortunes rested on every detail of their most personal life. The question of whether or not Arthur consummated his marriage was to become one of the most hotly debated issues in English history. The first report, long before the controversy, and long before anyone had reason to lie about it, came from Catherine's duenna. She declared that Catherine was still a virgin.

Ferdinand and Isabella were pleased. In the sixteenth century, the map of Europe was not yet firm; its national boundaries were not set. Italy was not a nation, and the separate Italian states were prey to the ambitions of both Spain and France. The Spanish monarchs wanted to conquer Italy before France did and they needed England to keep France too busy fighting in the north to invade in the south. Therefore they asked their ambassador to probe the possibility of marrying Catherine to Arthur's brother Henry, when he was old enough. For them it was important not to lose the English alliance.

For Henry VII the important thing was not to lose Catherine's dowry. When his wife, Elizabeth of York, died on her thirty-seventh birthday, Henry offered to marry his daughter-in-law himself. This would save a lot of time and bother, since the bride was already in his kingdom, and he already had half her dowry. It would, of course, require a papal dispensation, but popes were usually agreeable about royal marriages. However Isabella declined this match not because she was outraged—nothing royalty did was outrageous in those days—but because it was shortsighted. If Catherine married the forty-six-year-old monarch, she would probably not be queen for very long and at Henry's death the alliance would again be threatened. Ferdinand and Isabella wanted the son, not the father. They were gambling on a long reign and a long alliance.

Henry VII shrugged off the rebuff and began looking elsewhere for a wife, although he never did marry again. He agreed to have Catherine betrothed to Prince Henry, and the new marriage treaty was signed some fourteen months after Arthur's death. The wedding would be held when Henry was fifteen, as long as the balance of Catherine's dowry was in order. Both families agreed to ask the pope for a dispensation to permit the marriage, which would ordinarily be forbidden because Catherine had been married to Henry's brother.

By the time the dispensation was granted by Pope Julius II at the end of 1504, Isabella of Spain was dying, and with her death, the marriage plans foundered. Isabella had been queen of Castile; Ferdinand was king of Aragon. Their marriage had united Spain. But Isabella's crown was the more important of the two and her heir was not Ferdinand but their daughter, Joanna. Ferdinand of Aragon became a minor figure, and his daughter Catherine was no longer worthy of marriage to a future king of England.

Henry VII moved at once. On June 27, 1505, the day before the prince's fourteenth birthday, young Henry appeared before the king's council. As directed by his father, he protested his betrothal to Catherine on the grounds that it had been made while he was still a minor and said he would not be bound by it.

The following year Henry VII attempted to make his own Spanish match. Philip of Burgundy, the husband of Joanna of Castile, died suddenly. It was suspected that he had been poisoned by his father-in-law, Ferdinand. Joanna adored her husband; she went mad and refused to bury his body. Ferdinand immediately seized control of Castile, but Henry VII tried to win the rich province by offering to marry Joanna. Henry asked the Spanish ambassador to tell Ferdinand he would be such a good husband that Joanna would regain her sanity, and if she didn't the English wouldn't mind. Ferdinand, who had no intention of surrendering Castile, replied that he would be happy to have Henry marry his daughter if only he could persuade her to bury her previous husband.

All of this time Catherine of Aragon remained in England, and her position grew steadily worse. Henry did not want her to return to Spain because it meant giving back her dowry. Ferdinand did not want her back as long as there was any hope the new prince of Wales might marry her after all. But although she was useful as a pawn, neither her father nor her father-in-law would support her. She lived in humiliation and poverty, wearing torn dresses and eating rotten fish.

She was not permitted to see the prince of Wales, who grew to manhood not knowing whom he might marry, since one day it was a French princess and the next day it was Catherine again. Henry VII climbed onto his deathbed still plotting marriages and alliances that never took place.

By the end of 1508 Ferdinand had once again become a major power in Europe. Now Henry told his envoy in Spain to resume negotiations for a wedding between his son and Catherine. There was bitter wrangling over the remainder of the dowry, and Ferdinand kept his temper only because he knew that Henry was in the last stages of tuberculosis.

In April, 1509, Ferdinand finally lost patience. He demanded that the prince of Wales marry Catherine at once. If he did not, Catherine was to return to Spain and Henry had better not try to stop her.

The gauntlet had been flung by Ferdinand, but it was not picked up. By the time Ferdinand's letter reached England, Henry VII was dead.

# 2 ❧ Pastime with Good Company

ENRY VII died on April 21, 1509. When the heralds at his funeral cried, "The noble King Henry the Seventh is dead. God send the noble King Henry the Eighth long life!" they spoke for all England. The people rejoiced because the succession had passed without quarrel or bloodshed for the first time in over half a century. It had passed not only peacefully but to a paragon of princely virtues. Henry VII had been a wise and prudent king, but he was neither mourned nor missed. He had brought order to England and England to order, but he was crafty rather than gallant, a manipulator rather than a hero.

In contrast to his dour, waspish father, Henry VIII seemed to burst with color and life. He came to the throne just two months shy of his eighteenth birthday, the richest, best-looking, most virile monarch in Europe.

"His majesty," wrote one ambassador, "is the handsomest potentate I ever set eyes on; above the usual height, with an extremely fine calf to his leg; his complexion fair and bright, with auburn hair combed straight and short in the French fashion, and a round face so very beautiful that it would become a pretty woman. . . . He speaks French, English, Latin, and a little Italian; plays well on the lute and harpsichord, sings from the book at sight, draws the bow with greater strength than any man in England, and jousts marvellously."

Englishmen overreached themselves in searching for glowing phrases to enshrine their new king. Lord William Mountjoy, one of Henry's former tutors, wrote Erasmus: "What a hero he now shows himself, how wisely he behaves, what a lover he is of justice and goodness, what affection he bears to the learned. . . . Oh, my Erasmus, if you could see how all the world here is rejoicing in the possession of so great a prince. . . . Our king does not desire gold or gems or precious metals, but virtue, glory, immortality. I will give you an example. The other day he wished he was more learned. I said: 'That is not what we expect of your Grace, but that you will foster and encourage learned men.'

" 'Yea, surely,' said he, 'for indeed without them we should scarcely exist at all.'

"What more splendid saying could fall from the lips of a prince?"

Unfortunately, much as everyone admired Henry, no one admired him more than he admired himself. Those philosophers of the day who were called humanists, because they believed in man, expected a good and learned prince to rule wisely and well. "It is the duty of a prince to seek the public and not his own private advantage," wrote Erasmus. But this was a lesson Henry never learned, and since he had absolute power long after he had ceased to have absolute approval, there was no one who could teach it to him.

Henry began his reign by arresting two of his father's officials, Sir Richard Empson and Edmund Dudley. Empson and Dudley had preyed upon the people, extorting money for the old king, who had become increasingly greedy in his last years. Since their only crime had been to carry out his father's orders, Henry had them executed on false charges. The executions were immensely popular, but they quickly revealed a pattern that would be repeated frequently during Henry's long reign. The king would rid himself of servants who were no longer useful by judicial murder.

The first important personal decision facing the new king was the selection of a wife, which his father had made a lunatic's game ever since Arthur's death. Without hesitation Henry chose Catherine of Aragon. Henry VII was scarcely cold in his coffin when Henry VIII and Catherine were quietly married on June 11, 1509.

Henry explained his choice by saying that he was carrying out his father's deathbed wish; that it honored long-standing treaties; that since the pope had already granted a dispensation, "we could not, without offense to God, right, reason, and good conscience, do otherwise than as we have done." But these were formal reasons, in a formal letter to the regent of the Netherlands.

In a letter to Ferdinand, now his father-in-law, Henry wrote that Catherine's "eminent virtues daily more and more shine forth, blossom, and increase so much that, if we were still free, her we would yet choose for our wife before all others." Henry may have been fulfilling his father's wish, but he was also fulfilling his own. He married Catherine because he had fallen in love with her, possibly because she was forbidden to him for so many years. As for Catherine, who was suddenly raised from harassment and poverty to adoration and splendor, she wrote that she loved Henry "much more than myself."

On Sunday, June 24, four days before his eighteenth birthday, Henry was crowned king of England. Edward Hall, a contemporary chronicler, described the royal procession through the streets of London the day before the coronation. The handsome, auburn-haired king, who was over six feet tall, wore a robe of crimson velvet with ermine fur and a jacket of cloth of gold embroidered with diamonds, rubies, emeralds, pearls, and other rich stones.

Catherine sat "in her litter," wrote Hall, "borne by two white palfries . . . her person appareled in white satin embroidered, her hair hanging down to her back, of a very great length, beautiful and goodly to behold. . . ."

The next day, Henry and Catherine went to Westminster Abbey where, Hall wrote, "according to the sacred observance, and ancient custom, his Grace with the queen were anointed and crowned by the archbishop of Canterbury. . . . It was demanded of the people whether they would receive, obey, and take the same most noble prince for their king, who with great reverence, love, and desire said and cried, 'yea! yea!'"

The coronation over, the celebrations commenced, with feasting, jousts, tournaments, and pageants. As backdrop for the festivities, huge sets were built, with an artificial castle and gargoyles that spouted red and white wine. The coronation celebrations were interrupted by the inconsiderate death of Henry's grandmother, Margaret Beaufort, but they resumed as soon as possible. A month after the coronation, Catherine wrote to her father, "Our time is ever passed in continual feasts."

There was no special reason, nor did Henry need any. He was eighteen years old, healthy, happy, adored, powerful, and rich. Henry VII had been lavish on occasion, but only on occasion. He was a poor adventurer who had painfully earned and hoarded his wealth, so he knew the value of it and died the richest king in Christendom. Henry VIII was very much the spoiled son of the self-made man. Never having had the responsibility of earning money, he spent it as he pleased. Never having had to earn the responsibility of being king, he governed England as he pleased.

For Henry VII being king meant work. For Henry VIII being king meant self-indulgence. It meant doing what he wanted, and what he wanted to do was hunt, sing, dance, joust, gamble, feast, and adorn himself with satin, velvet, gold, and diamonds. "His fingers were one mass of jewelled rings," wrote one visitor.

Henry made his life style lyrically clear in one of the first ballads he composed:

> *Pastance [pastime] with good company*
> *I love and shall until I die*
> *Grudge who will, but none deny,*
> *So God be pleased this life will I*
> > *For my pastance,*
> > *Hunt, sing, and dance,*
> > *My heart is set;*
> > *All goodly sport*
> > *To my comfort*
> > *Who shall me let?*

Who shall me let? Who shall stop me, asked Henry, for I am the king.

While the young monarch was reveling in his father's money, there was a kingdom to rule. Fortunately Henry's wise and pious grandmother had lived just long enough to help him choose a council, mostly made up of men who had served his father. It was these graybeards who did the drudgery and ran the kingdom while Henry frolicked.

The land over which Henry reigned, but did not yet rule, had a population of about three million, in both England and Wales. Scotland was an independent and unfriendly kingdom, allied with England's traditional enemy, France. In theory the king of England was also lord of Ireland, but only a small strip of land north of Dublin was under English control. The rest of the country was largely untamed, with the Irish nobles in constant quarrel with England and one another.

In England, though, thanks to Henry VII, there was peace and prosperity. About 90 percent of the people lived off the land, although much of it was now used for sheep grazing and English commerce thrived on wool and cloth. Exporting these items was profitable, and the leading market was the Netherlands.

Towns and villages dotted the English countryside, each with its farmers, its craftsmen, and its merchants. But the most important city in all England was London, with perhaps seventy-five thousand inhabitants. Because the streets of London were narrow and crooked, the Thames River served as a main highway, and barges were rowed up and down the river, bearing men, materials, and messages from one important center of the city to the other.

The people of London made their money from either trade

or craft, and the city was thronged with tailors, grocers, skinners, and cloth and clothing makers. The country's precious metals also found their way there, and on one street alone there were fifty-two goldsmith shops.

Beyond the city, at Westminster, was the seat of the English government. The king usually lived at Westminster at least part of the year, and Parliament often met there, when it met at all. For Parliament sat only when summoned by the king, usually because he needed money or special legislation. Members were elected by wealthy landowners, and elections were usually not contested. The common people could not vote, and therefore Parliament was not their voice in government. It was just a body of oligarchs who did the king's will, and the people dreaded when a Parliament was called because it usually meant more taxes.

The king controlled not only the executive and legislative branches of government but the judicial as well. Although there were ordinary law courts, the Court of Star Chamber was the real judicial power in England.

Thus all the functions of government rested with the monarch. No one branch could check, balance, or counter another because it had no real power independent of the king. All that was government in England resided in one man, who was not chosen for the job but born to it. Anyone who objected to the king's rule could either be silent and suffer, or rebel and die. There was no middle course.

At the beginning of his reign, Henry tended to rely on his wife Catherine when an important decision was due. She was five and one-half years older than he was and better educated, and her years as a widow had taught her much about dealing with kings. For two years before her second marriage, and for a time afterward, she was actually the accredited Spanish ambassador at court.

Ferdinand had agreed to give his youngest daughter to England in order to gain an ally against France and he quickly found the opportunity to make use of his innocent young son-in-law. Late in 1508 the European powers had agreed to bury the hatchet long enough to plunge it into the back of Venice, a wealthy but weak Italian state. King Louis XII of France had done this so expeditiously that Ferdinand was annoyed with the French king for getting to the loot ahead of him. Ferdinand decided to drive the French out of Italy; he also had his eye on the small kingdom of Navarre, which lay between France and Spain.

Ferdinand needed Henry to divert France with war while Spain was seizing what it wanted. It took no effort to persuade Henry that the French were his enemies, since the English had spent 116 years, from 1337 to 1453, unsuccessfully trying to conquer France. All they clung to was the port of Calais, yet kings of England still called themselves kings of France as well, a title that was sheer puffery since France had its own monarch.

Henry VII had gone to war only once in his twenty-four-year reign, and that was primarily a feint in order to extort a ransom. But Henry VIII had barely warmed the throne when he began to speak of war with France. War was as natural for him as it had been unnatural for his father. It combined all the elements Henry VIII so loved: expense, pomp, noise, and action. It was sport, a tournament abroad that was all the more exciting because the victims were real.

But even in preparing for war, Henry left all the details to others and concentrated on his amusements. Some English bishops complained to the Spanish ambassador that the king "does not care to occupy himself with anything but the pleasures of his age. All other affairs he neglects."

If Henry found life one continual game, Catherine had more serious and painful obligations. Within a year of their marriage she gave birth to a stillborn girl. Deeply religious, she called it "the will of God" and soon became pregnant again. On January 1, 1511, she gave birth to a son. England rejoiced; the crown would pass peacefully to the next generation. The infant was christened Henry and named prince of Wales.

The celebrations for the child exceeded anything that had been seen before, even at Henry's court. The king was in such high humor that at one point he offered his guests the gold ornaments on his clothing. Seeing this, wrote Hall, "the common people . . . ran to the king and stripped him to his hose and doublet, and all his companions likewise. . . ." The king's guard had to drive the people back. Then the king and queen had a great banquet, said Hall, "and all these hurts were turned to laughing and game."

The laughter soon turned to tears, however, when the infant prince died. Hall wrote that Catherine, "like a natural woman, made much lamentation." Henry was crushed with sorrow, but not for long. The number of miscarriages, stillborn children, and infant deaths was extraordinarily high. Children died easily in those days, but they came easily too. He and Catherine would have more, and they would live.

Consoled by this thought Henry turned back to the war that

was pending with France. Wars were not usually fought in winter, but they could be comfortably plotted then. In November, 1511, Henry and Ferdinand agreed to attack France in the spring. The war that followed was England's first significant foreign adventure in more than half a century. Yet in its time it bore no name but Wolsey's War, after a member of the king's council named Thomas Wolsey.

Thomas Wolsey was born in the town of Ipswich in the year 1471. The exact date was not recorded, for no one would take notice of the birth of a butcher's son. The elder Wolsey had been born low and raised himself through hard work and energy. He earned enough money to make his son a gentleman, and Thomas Wolsey, bright beyond his years, was sent to Oxford, where he won his bachelor of arts degree at the age of fifteen.

While Henry Tudor was establishing himself on the throne of England, Wolsey was earning his master's degree and teaching. But Thomas Wolsey was a man with his eye on the future, and he saw no future as a teacher. He was intelligent, articulate, and he had an amazing capacity for details. He would go far, if he found the right route. He decided to go by way of Rome.

The church in Catholic England offered hope to young men of low birth and high ambition. Religion had nothing to do with it, for both church and churchmen had forfeited God for mammon. Reforming preacher John Colet was soon to denounce the church as "foul and deformed" and complain that "the magnates of the church are busied in vile and earthly things. . . ." But vile and earthly things were precisely what attracted Wolsey. The church could lead to money and power, for high churchmen were among the chief councillors of the king. This was a convenience for both sides. The church provided the councillors' income, which spared the king's purse, but in return it won strong influence in state affairs.

Wolsey was ordained in 1498 and given his first parish. It was customary at the time for a priest of promise to take the revenues of his parish and tend to temporal matters, while assigning the spiritual duties to a curate. By the end of 1501, still pocketing the income from his first parish and others that he never even saw, Wolsey became chaplain to Henry Deane, archbishop of Canterbury, the most important churchman in England.

After Deane died in 1503, Wolsey served the lord deputy of Calais, the English-held port in France. There he learned to be an administrator and a clerk and to deal with details that most men found numbing. He did his work so well that he was recommended to the court, and in 1505 Thomas Wolsey became chaplain to Henry VII. Henry Tudor cared more for a job well done than for a man well born. At Henry's court, even the son of a butcher could make his mark.

In the spring of 1508, Henry sent Wolsey on a diplomatic errand to Maximilian, the Holy Roman Emperor, who was in the Netherlands at the time. Wolsey prepared well for this journey. He received his final instructions from Henry at Richmond Palace at four in the afternoon. He had a barge waiting for him, and because he had chosen the hour well, the wind and tides enabled him to reach Gravesend in three hours. He had already arranged to have horses waiting for him at Gravesend and other stops, and thus he was able to gallop into the port of Dover the next morning to catch the channel ferry just as it was leaving. He was in Calais by noon and rode directly to the emperor's residence that after-noon.

Maximilian saw him at once and had a reply for Henry the next morning. Wolsey sped home and was back at Richmond Palace within seventy hours.

The following morning Wolsey waited outside the king's bedchamber for Henry to go to mass. When Henry saw his chaplain he was annoyed. "Why have you not passed on your journey?" he asked.

This was the moment Wolsey had been savoring. His answer was ready: "Sire, if it may stand with your Highness' pleasure, I have already been with the Emperor and dispatched your affairs, I trust to your Grace's liking."

Henry thanked him for his "good and speedy exploit." As a reward Wolsey was given the income of several more parishes. He was also raised to the position of royal almoner, the priest in charge of doling out alms, or charity, for the king, although he was used for more complex assignments as well.

When Henry VIII succeeded his father, Wolsey remained at court as royal almoner and soon became an important adviser. He was twenty years older than the young monarch, or old enough to seem fatherly without being so old as to seem forbidding. By 1511 Wolsey was a member of the king's council.

Wolsey rose rapidly not only because he was more capable than the other councillors, but because he understood Henry better. While the others begged the king to spend less time in tourneys and more time in ruling, Wolsey did the opposite.

A contemporary wrote: "so fast as the other councillors advised the king to leave his pleasure, and to attend to the affairs of his realm, so busily did the almoner persuade him to the contrary; which delighted him much, and caused him to have the greater affection to the almoner."

Unlike his father, Henry VIII wanted the glory of being king without the burden. The burden he would leave to men like Thomas Wolsey.

# 3 ❦ A Somewhat Necessary War

WHEN HENRY decided to invade France in 1512, the task of preparing the arms and army fell upon Wolsey's shoulders. Command of the English force was given to the marquis of Dorset. On Ferdinand's advice Dorset was to land with ten thousand men at Fuentarrabia, a town on the southern border of Guienne. Guienne was a strip of territory in southwest France which had once belonged to England, and Ferdinand had promised to help Henry reconquer it.

It never seems to have occurred to Henry or Wolsey or Dorset that southern France was an odd place to choose for an English invasion. Henry simply accepted it because he trusted his father-in-law and because he hoped to take Guienne. But this was an age when duplicity was the highest form of statesmanship. Ferdinand cared not a fig for Henry or Guienne. He wanted Dorset's army not for an invasion of France but to protect his own men while they took Navarre.

Henry rode personally to Southampton to bid his army godspeed as it set off on its adventure. The men sailed on June 3 and within the week had landed on the Spanish coast and marched inland to Fuentarrabia to wait for the Spanish army. They waited and waited in the blazing Spanish sun, but the army that was supposed to meet them was marching on Navarre, shielded from French attack by the English.

For three months Dorset's men sweated out the hot and rainy Spanish summer without tents to shield them, without enough food, and without enough beer. The soldiers turned, in their thirst, to the unaccustomed Spanish wine, and they became sick and rebellious. They struck for more pay and voted to return to England. Henry ordered his army to winter in Spain, but the men mobbed their officers shouting, "Home! Home!" A seething Henry told Ferdinand to cut the throat of any man who disobeyed, but it was too late. The men had already sailed for England, their officers trailing behind them.

Henry's first war had cost the English a small fortune and some two thousand men, all of them lost to dysentery and disease rather than to the enemy. It also cost Henry his pride, for his men had mutinied and slunk home against orders. Both Henry and Wolsey were humiliated in all of Europe. Margaret, regent of the Netherlands, wondered aloud if the English had "so long abstained from war, they lack experience from disuse."

A hot-blooded twenty-one-year-old king and a councillor with great ambitions could not bear to have Europe's royalty laughing up their embroidered sleeves. England's honor would have to be avenged in the only acceptable manner—by another war.

The slippery Ferdinand, who was responsible for the disaster, complained loudly about the cowardice of the English troops.

He was just coming to join them when they left, he said. Henry and his father-in-law made fresh plans to invade France together in 1513, Ferdinand from the south, Henry across the channel. So that the English army would not retreat this time, the king himself would lead it.

With the threat of a joint invasion as a bargaining point, Ferdinand now went to the French and offered to negotiate a temporary truce, which would give him enough time to secure Navarre without French intervention. The more warlike Henry behaved, the more anxious the French were to make peace with Ferdinand. At about the same time the Spanish ambassador in London was solemnly agreeing to a treaty which bound Spain to go to war against France, Spanish and French representatives were solemnly agreeing to a year's truce everywhere but in Italy.

Henry was furious when he learned of the betrayal, but Ferdinand insisted it was all a misunderstanding. In an age of rogues, the Spanish king was a master. Louis XII of France once complained that Ferdinand had deceived him twice. "He lies, the sot!" boasted Ferdinand. "I have deceived him five times!"

Henry forgave Ferdinand for this second betrayal, partly because of his innocence and partly because the Spanish king was father of a wife he loved. Anyway, Ferdinand's truce with France would not bar English action. Henry decided to proceed with the invasion, which would give him a second chance to show the stuff of English honor. Again all the details fell on Wolsey, but this time there would be no mishaps; there would be tents and there would be beer.

There would also be some forty thousand men, and so large an army had never before left England. No government office existed to make the arrangements, which suited Wolsey perfectly since he climbed the executive ladder by filling in missing rungs. Wolsey spent the early months of 1513 worrying over the details, large and small, of the invasion of France. He ordered the beer, the beef, the bacon, and the biscuits, and even saw to the arms. Until the time of the Tudors, the English had fought mainly with longbows. But these were considered very primitive, since they killed only one man at a time. Progress brought with it the use of cannon, and English foundries were put to work casting the new weapons. Henry placed a special order for a dozen huge cannon, each to be named after one of the apostles.

However not everyone agreed that Henry's mission was holy. The humanist preacher John Colet said pointedly that "when men out of hatred and ambition fight with and destroy one another, they fight under the banner, not of Christ, but the Devil."

But Henry brushed aside such criticism or charmed his critics, including Colet. Ships were built and launched, including the flagship *Henry Grace à Dieu*, commonly known as the *Great Harry*. The king and supreme head of the Royal Navy was so proud of his new toy that the day the ship was launched, he stood on the deck blowing commands on an enormous jeweled gold whistle.

The cost of the saintly cannon, the ships, and the provisions was enormous. People grumbled when prices rose in England, forced up by the demands of the army, although their anger was directed not at the king, but at the butcher's son who sat by his side, taxing and spending. One of the reasons they grumbled was that no one seemed to know why this particular war was being fought. But Henry knew. It was "to recover the realm of France, his very true patrimony and inheritance, and to reduce the same to his obedience." He also called it a "just, holy, and somewhat necessary war."

This somewhat necessary war began with a somewhat unnecessary defeat. In April, 1513, an English fleet set off to sweep the channel of French ships so the king and his army could sail safely to Calais. In a moment of bravado, the English admiral, Sir Edward Howard, led an attack on the French fleet in four small rowboats. He boarded the French admiral's galley, but was cut down and thrust overboard by French pikes. It was foolish but heroic, and the English stopped complaining about the cost of the war and began to thrill to the challenge.

Henry and his main force sailed for Calais on June 30. Before he left England, he took measures to protect his throne by executing Edmund de la Pole, the Yorkist claimant. The old quarrel between Lancaster and York was not so dead that it could not be resurrected, particularly since Henry and Catherine had still not produced an heir.

The English landed in Calais with bag and baggage intact. The soldiers had their beer and the nobles had their servants, their silk cushions, and their silver spoons. The man who made it all possible was the king's almoner, Thomas Wolsey. Wolsey had sailed to France with Henry, showing his priestly humility by wearing a simple gown amid the gorgeous robes and riding a humble mule amid the prancing chargers. But the simple almoner was attended by two hundred men, and it was he who stood closest to the king and made the decisions for him.

Henry's campaign against the French moved in slow and stately fashion, as befitted a just and holy war. Henry did not leave Calais to join his army in enemy territory until July 21. Early in August, Maximilian, the Holy Roman Emperor, rode into Henry's camp dressed in modest black. Perpetually short of cash, Maximilian offered himself and his troops to Henry, for a fee. Henry accepted, honored to have an emperor in his service. But just as Ferdinand had persuaded Henry to invade France from the south, where Ferdinand's interests lay, Maximilian persuaded Henry to begin his conquest by taking Thérouanne and Tournai, two fortified French towns which threatened territory belonging to the emperor's grandson.

Thérouanne fell on August 22, the first French city captured by the English since the Hundred Years' War. But the French scarcely troubled to defend themselves, and the only action Henry saw was when the English routed a detachment of French cavalry in what was called the Battle of the Spurs. Henry was held back until it was safe, then he was permitted to charge after the re-treating enemy and take some prisoners.

From Thérouanne, which Maximilian ordered razed to the ground, Henry moved on to besiege Tournai. It took Henry eight days to capture the city and three weeks to celebrate his victory. By then it was autumn and time to return home. The war was a personal triumph for Henry, for although he had accomplished little, he had at least erased the failures of the previous summer. It was also a triumph for Wolsey, for this time the army had not lacked for shelter or beer.

While Henry was in France, England was threatened by a nearer enemy. As soon as Henry sailed for the continent, the Scots prepared to invade. Henry had left his pregnant wife

Catherine to rule in his absence, and she calmly raised an army to meet the Scottish attack. She wrote Wolsey that she was "horribly busy with making standards, banners, and badges."

Late in August, Henry's brother-in-law, King James IV of Scotland, crossed the Tweed River with an enormous army. The Scots and the English met at Flodden Edge on September 9. By nightfall some ten thousand Scots had perished, including their king and most of his nobles. Although Flodden was not his personal victory, Henry was more than willing to revel in it. He had captured two French cities, and now the Scottish threat had been destroyed, at least for a time. England was becoming a formidable power and Henry would leave a great kingdom to his son. But what son? In September Catherine had a boy who died either at birth or shortly after. When Henry sailed home to harvest his triumphs, he was still without an heir.

The king spent the winter of 1513–14 at the usual feasts and revels, taking a moment here and there to plan another invasion of France in the spring with his father-in-law and Maximilian. But his two allies were only bluffing, hoping to force France to surrender her Italian conquests to them. In February, 1514, Henry was ill with what was probably smallpox. He was even more ill later that spring when, as he prepared for the joint invasion, he learned that Ferdinand and Maximilian had made a truce with France.

It was the third time Ferdinand had deceived him. At first Henry exercised his fury on his wife, Ferdinand's daughter. It was rumored that he threatened to divorce her, even though she was pregnant again at the time. The child, a boy, died soon after birth.

Then Henry realized that more was at stake than a domestic quarrel. If he was going to survive in the European jungle, he would have to lie, deal, and dissemble like the others. "I do not see any faith in the world save in me only," he told an ambassador. Then he added characteristically, "Therefore, God Almighty, who knows this, prospers my affairs."

Henry decided to settle the score with Ferdinand and Maximilian. If they made a truce with France, he would go one better; he would make a marriage alliance. The king of France, Louis XII, had just lost his wife. Henry had a younger sister, Mary, who was betrothed to Charles, the grandson and heir of both Maximilian and Ferdinand. Henry would punish the two old schemers by breaking the engagement and marrying Mary to the king of France.

Mary was eighteen years old and one of the prettiest princesses in Europe. Louis was fifty-two, sickly, gouty, pockmarked, and toothless. But when it came to affairs of state, Henry held personal feelings cheaply, as long as they were not his own.

Louis wed Mary in October, 1514, and the shock was so great that the doddering old king died eleven weeks later. He was succeeded by his twenty-year-old nephew, who would reign as Francis I. Francis was as hotblooded and as vain as Henry, and the history of Europe for the next thirty years would revolve upon the rivalry of Henry, Francis, and a third monarch who had not yet taken his throne. For Henry it was on a very personal level.

"The king of France, is he as tall as I am?" Henry demanded of a Venetian visitor one day. The Venetian said there was little difference.

"Is he as stout?" Henry persisted. The Venetian said no.

"What sort of legs has he?" Henry asked. The Venetian said "spare," for Francis' legs were thin. Then Henry opened his doublet and put his hand on his thigh. "Look here," he boasted, "and I also have a good calf to my leg."

While Henry was worrying over who had the sturdier calf, the politics of the situation with France and elsewhere was slipping out of his hands, if it had ever been there, and into the receptive grasp of Thomas Wolsey. Wolsey had proved himself during the invasion of 1513 and thereafter. Nothing was too dirty, too difficult, or too trivial for him. One of his aides marveled that he could write letters from four in the morning until four in the afternoon without once leaving his table. He was loyal, ambitious, and dedicated; an ideal servant for an indifferent king, particularly since the church paid his salary.

When Henry wanted to reward Wolsey, he gave him another bishopric, for although bishops were approved by the pope, they were proposed by the king. In this way Wolsey's wealth kept pace with his power. By 1514 he was archbishop of York and pressing hard for a cardinal's hat. On August 12 Henry wrote Pope Leo X asking him to make his "most secret counsellor" a cardinal. The pope hesitated for several reasons; one of them was the suspicion that Wolsey had had the preceding archbishop of York murdered.

Then, in the summer of 1515, Francis invaded Italy. The pope felt threatened; Wolsey suggested slyly that if he were a cardinal it would help "make the king [Henry] fast to the pope." He warned that without Henry's help, the pope might be in great danger. By September, Wolsey was a cardinal.

As cardinal the commoner from Ipswich took precedence over all the nobles of the kingdom. When his red hat arrived from Rome, it was placed on the high altar at Westminster Abbey for four days, and England's nobility was forced to genuflect to the hat and to the cardinal's empty seat.

Wolsey was now the leading churchman in England, and before the year was out he was also the leading statesman. On Christmas eve, 1515, Wolsey became lord chancellor, or, in effect, prime minister. As cardinal, Wolsey's loyalty was to the pope. As lord chancellor, his loyalty was to the king. As long as the interests of king and pope were identical, Wolsey was safe. But if the two ever clashed, Wolsey would be crushed in between.

On February 18, 1516, Catherine gave birth again. The child was only a girl, but at least it lived and was christened Mary. When the Venetian ambassador said a boy would have been better, Henry replied jovially, "We are both young. If it was a daughter this time, by the grace of God, the sons will follow." And like any other proud father he boasted that "this baby never cries."

For Henry a daughter meant only that sons were possible. He did not seriously consider Mary his heir. Only once in English history, in the year 1139, had the daughter of a king tried to claim the throne. She was never crowned, and her attempt to rule plunged the country into nineteen years of civil war. This would not do. To keep the Tudors on the throne, sons were needed.

Although Catherine undoubtedly also wished for sons, she did not see why Mary might not rule England someday. Catherine's mother, Isabella of Castile, was one of the greatest monarchs of her age, far superior to her husband, Ferdinand of Aragon.

By 1516 Ferdinand was Henry's ally once again. Francis had conquered northern Italy with a spectacular victory at the battle of Marignano, near Milan, and Henry was so jealous he almost wept. He dropped all thought of a French alliance for the time and turned back to his father-in-law and Maximilian. Once more plans were made to invade France and to drive the French out of Italy. The brunt of the fighting in Italy would be borne by twenty thousand Swiss mercenaries, to be paid by England.

Ferdinand died that January, but the assault on France was pressed, in Henry's imagination if nowhere else. The Swiss marched toward Milan, and Maximilian followed with his army. But the night before the attack, Maximilian had a vision. Spirits from the next world warned him to turn back, he said, and he promptly obeyed, leaving the Swiss to fight alone. Actually the vision he had was apparently of a bribe from the other side.

The Swiss now demanded more money from England. As soon as they got it, they went home. The entire campaign was a rollicking fiasco, with Henry playing the goat and paying the bills. Yet he still wanted to invade France, even if he had to do it himself. His councillors managed to cool him down by convincing him that it would cost too much, and the people were already bitterly complaining about the money wasted trying to evict the French from Italy.

With Ferdinand's death, the new ruler of Spain was his sixteen-year-old grandson Charles, the son of Ferdinand's daughter, Joanna the Mad, and Maximilian's son, Philip of Burgundy. Charles was a serious youth with pale blue eyes, bowed legs, and the jutting chin that came to be known as the Habsburg jaw. He was the youngest of the three monarchs who would dominate the first half of the sixteenth century in Europe. Unlike Henry and Francis he was neither lusty nor impetuous. He was so slow and solemn that the impish Maximilian said, "We're certainly glad that our boy Charles takes so much pleasure in hunting, otherwise people might suspect he was illegitimate." When Ferdinand died Charles ruled Spain; when Maximilian died he would rule the Habsburg lands as well.

Both Henry and Francis knew Charles would be a valuable ally. While Henry was trying to get Charles to sign an anti-French treaty, Charles signed a treaty with Francis at Noyon in which he agreed, among other things, to marry the French king's daughter.

Maximilian assured the English that he thought this treaty was shameful, and if they would pay his expenses to the Netherlands, where his grandson lived, he would do something about it. The English paid and Maximilian did do something about it. When he saw Charles he cackled, "My son, you are going to cheat the French, and I am going to cheat the English." Having already been bribed by the English, Maximilian took another bribe from the French and joined in the treaty of Noyon. Henry's anti-French policy had cost several fortunes and gained him nothing but repeated humiliation.

While Henry and Wolsey were stumbling through the barnyards of European diplomacy, and being plucked clean by the Holy Roman Emperor and others, they were also having their difficulties at home. The people of London felt that the king favored foreigners at their expense. It was true that he had done all he could to encourage foreign trade. He had even loaned money to foreign merchants, who used it to buy goods in England, thus competing with domestic merchants. English craftsmen and apprentices, many of them out of work, looked with anger and envy at the hundreds of foreign tradesmen thronging the city, prosperous and privileged.

At Easter, 1517, a preacher aroused the Londoners with a sermon against foreigners. Word went out that on May Day the Londoners would slaughter all aliens in the city. Henry was not in London and he made no move to come. Wolsey, however, called the mayor to him and said, "We are informed that your young and riotous people will rise up and distress the strangers. Hear ye of no such thing!"

The cardinal called in thirteen hundred men to keep order, which had the opposite effect of making the city more tense. On the night of April 30, a man tried to disperse a crowd of apprentices. They refused to move. He seized one by the arm, and immediately the rallying cry of the apprentices was heard, "Clubs! Prentices!" The streets were soon jammed with mobs of workers who attacked houses where foreigners lived, threatened to kill Wolsey, and forced the mayor to open the jails and free the prisoners.

The incident became known as Evil May Day. No one was killed but many were injured. The ringleaders of the plot were hanged, drawn, and quartered, and over four hundred persons were arrested. But sentiment in London favored the rioters, and the people complained about official brutality.

Since both Wolsey and Henry liked theatrics, they decided to settle the matter with a good show. The danger over, the king came to London with three queens: his wife Catherine; his sister Margaret, widow of the king of Scotland; and his sister Mary, widow of the king of France.

He went to Westminster Hall with his council and the lords of the kingdom. According to the chronicler Hall, who was present, "The king commanded that all the prisoners should be brought forth. Then came in the poor younglings and old false knaves, bound in ropes, all along one after another, in their shirts, and every one [with] a halter about his neck, to the number of four hundred men and eleven women."

Queen Catherine knelt before the king to ask him to spare the lives of those "whose riot had spilled the blood of her Spanish countrymen." Henry appeared to be unmoved. The other two queens also knelt before him; he was still unmoved.

Then the cardinal begged the king's compassion, but Henry was unyielding. The prisoners fell to their knees crying, "Mercy, gracious lord, mercy!" At that point the cardinal also fell to his knees, and Henry finally granted a royal pardon. Hall wrote that "it was a fine sight to see each man take the halter from his neck and fling it in the air; and how they jumped for joy, making such signs of rejoicing as became people who had escaped from extreme peril."

The year 1517 not only saw the Evil May Day riot in London, but a severe outbreak of the disease known as the "sweating sickness," a form of influenza. It was first brought to England by the French mercenaries who came with Henry Tudor in 1485. On the continent the disease was a fairly mild one, but in England, where there was no resistance to it, it was merciless. It struck so rapidly that, as Hall wrote, a man might be "merry at dinner and dead at supper." The sweat was mysterious not only because of its rapid, malevolent course but because, unlike most epidemics, it had the impudence to attack the healthy and wealthy rather than the poor and sick.

There was no way to ward off the disease except to flee from an infected area, so Henry fled. He moved from palace to palace, while one man remained in London to keep the government functioning. This was Thomas Cardinal Wolsey. In June Wolsey fell victim to the sweat and his many enemies rejoiced. He survived, but suffered another attack in August. Many of his servants died, but Wolsey lived to receive the thanks of a grateful king.

The cardinal's dogged devotion to duty, in sickness and in health, enthralled Henry. Here was a man he could rely upon. And soon an ambassador was reporting, "The king takes his pleasure, and leaves to the cardinal the whole government of the realm." And one bishop remarked of Wolsey, "We shall have to deal with the cardinal, who is not cardinal, but king."

# 4 ~ King Wolsey

A S CHIEF and only executive, Wolsey asserted his authority
in every area of English life. He continued the work
begun by Henry VII of establishing a strong central
government in England. He kept the accounts of the treasury and
insisted that even the king record how his money was spent. He
spied on everyone in the kingdom, including the queen. He opened
the mail of both Englishmen and foreigners, and he was not
beyond threatening ambassadors with prison and the rack if they
did not do what he wanted.

Parliament was still a weak and indifferent political force, summoned only when money or special legislation was needed. It met
just once while Wolsey was lord chancellor. Legislation he drafted
for the last Parliament that met before he received his position revealed his mania for dictating every aspect of English life. One of
his measures kept wages down. Another kept the middle class
down. The butcher's son who had risen to rule decided that the
humble must remain so. His Act of Apparel decreed what men of
each class could wear and eat. Gentlemen could have three dishes

at a meal. Knights of the Garter could have six. The cardinal was entitled to nine. Fortunately, this did not work any hardship on the poor, who did not have that much to eat anyway.

Wolsey controlled all three branches of government, executive, legislative, and judicial. As lord chancellor, he presided over the Court of Star Chamber. The Venetian ambassador wrote that Wolsey "has the reputation of being extremely just; he favors the people exceedingly, and especially the poor, hearing their suits and seeking to dispatch them instantly." It was not so much a love for the poor that motivated this equity as a hatred for the nobility; like Henry VII, Wolsey used the Star Chamber to crush their power. The nobles hated him for this, and they also hated him because he was an upstart, a commoner who had been raised above them. Both nobles and commoners were offended by the excesses of his ego.

When Wolsey presided over the Star Chamber, four days a week, each journey to and from the court was a state procession. Dressed in fine crimson satin robes, with sable trim at the throat, Wolsey rode a mule, as became a humble churchman. But the mule was draped in red velvet, and the saddle had gold stirrups. Wolsey was always preceded by attendants carrying two great gold crosses, which led one of his legion of enemies to comment that "one cross is insufficient to atone for his sins." Other attendants bore the symbols of his authority, the great seal of England and his cardinal's hat. In the unlikely event that someone could miss this parade, ushers marched in front of Wolsey crying, "Make way for my lord cardinal!"

Wolsey not only made his own way through the government of England but through the church as well. Because the church was a career rather than a calling for him, he wanted to rise to the top. In 1518, Pope Leo X wrote that he wanted to send a legate, or representative, to England to discuss a papal plan wherein the princes of Europe would agree to a five-year truce during which they would fight the Turks instead of each other. Wolsey coolly let the pope's letter go unanswered.

Finally the pope said he was sending Cardinal Lorenzo Campeggio to England as his legate. But Campeggio got no farther than Calais. At that point, Wolsey finally replied to the pope. With Henry's consent, he wrote that the papal legate would not be permitted to enter England unless Wolsey was made a legate also. It was blackmail and it worked.

Wolsey was eventually named legate for life, which made him the pope's permanent representative in England, with the right to decide certain religious matters without consulting Rome. It also gave Wolsey the right to reform the church, which he knew was necessary. What he ignored was the fact that he embodied almost all that was wrong with it.

Essentially the problem was that the church cared more about worldly matters than spiritual ones, and no one illustrated this better than Cardinal Wolsey, the lord chancellor of England. Priests and monks overlooked their vows of chastity; Wolsey had a mistress who bore him a son and a daughter. Churchmen ignored their flocks and instead sought income and honor; Wolsey rarely said mass and rarely or never saw his bishoprics.

Monasteries and churchmen amassed enormous amounts of land and wealth to the detriment of the people, but no one surpassed Wolsey for greed. In addition to what he received from the bishoprics he never visited, he took fees for services to private

individuals, as well as pensions and grants from both Francis and
Charles.

Wolsey urged a simple and holy life upon the church, while
he built himself a palace at Hampton Court that was the largest
building erected in England since the time of the Roman conquest.
Rather than sleep on a monklike board, the cardinal rested on a
bed with eight mattresses.

Although Wolsey's palace beggared anything the king owned,
one of the things that disturbed the righteous cardinal was the
wealth of the monasteries in England. Some monasteries still performed useful functions, such as sheltering travelers and feeding
beggars, but in others, the monks would not work for themselves,
let alone anyone else. One monastery had thirty monks and eighty-
six servants.

Wolsey rose from his eight mattresses in wrath and ordered
the monasteries to reject worldly comforts. He was largely ignored.
He then proceeded to dissolve twenty-two monasteries and three
nunneries, and to use the proceeds to found a college at Oxford
University and a school in his home town of Ipswich.

Wolsey was not the first man in England to dissolve monasteries; both Henry VI and Henry VII had done so in order to
found colleges and hospitals. All of the monasteries Wolsey suppressed had twelve members or less. But there was some opposition
to the move, because those who lived near the monasteries benefited
from their charity, so some of the people fought off Wolsey's
agents when they came.

The agents were John Allen and Thomas Cromwell. It was
said that both men, particularly Cromwell, took bribes in order to
overlook houses that had been marked for extinction. Although

44

Cromwell's work did not make him loved, it made him invaluable. The time would come when Henry could use such a man.

For the moment, though, Henry did not need Cromwell because he had Wolsey. Although the king was intelligent and capable enough, he left everything to the cardinal. "Writing is to me somewhat tedious and painful," he wrote Wolsey once, and so the cardinal prepared state papers and Henry signed them, often without reading them first.

The whole business of kingship was tedious and painful to Henry, who was still only in his twenties. He watched Catherine grow old and ugly bearing him dead children and turned to other women. "The king," wrote one ambassador, "cares for nothing but girls and hunting." He hunted for as long as seventeen or eighteen hours a day and an Englishman commented, "He spares no pains to convert the sport of hunting into a martyrdom." "He devotes himself to accomplishments and amusements day and night," observed a papal official, "is intent on nothing else, and leaves business to Wolsey, who rules everything." The Venetian ambassador reported that when he first came to England, Wolsey would say, "His Majesty will do so and so." This changed to "We shall do so and so." By 1519 the cardinal was saying, "I shall do so and so."

The year before, Pope Leo had proclaimed his five-year truce and crusade. England was not interested in the Turks, but since it had failed to initiate a good war with France, it would settle for a good peace. If there was going to be peace, however, it would not be the pope's but Wolsey's.

For most of 1518 Wolsey worked at altering the pope's plan to suit his own grander scheme, and he succeeded. On October 2

England and France signed the Treaty of London, which bound them, the other great powers of Europe, and twenty minor ones, to perpetual peace. All disputes would be settled by arbitration, and anyone who broke the peace would be punished by collective action. It was not the first attempt to bring peace to Europe, nor would it be the last. As perpetual peaces go, it fared reasonably well. It lasted thirty months.

The other great powers signed the Treaty of London afterward. Meanwhile France and England signed separate treaties. Tournai was returned to France for a ransom that was far less than what it cost Henry to conquer it, and the king's infant daughter was betrothed to Francis' infant son.

To complete the reconciliation between England and France, it was decided that their two young monarchs must meet. The meeting was planned for the summer of 1519, but it was delayed because on a cold day in January of that year the Holy Roman Emperor went hunting. Maximilian caught a chill and died a few days later. His grandson Charles, already king of Spain, now inherited the Habsburg lands as well.

Although the possessions of the Habsburgs went to Charles, the title of Holy Roman Emperor did not. It was not a hereditary honor but an elective one, which carried with it the burden of trying to rule the German states. The German princes who chose the emperor made certain the office did not become hereditary because each time a new election was held they made a fortune in bribes and concessions from the contestants.

The election of 1519 was especially profitable because there were three contenders, Charles, Francis, and Henry. Henry was encouraged not only by his own driving ego, which persuaded him that the most honored title in Christendom rightly belonged to its most gracious prince, but also by the pope. The title Holy Roman Emperor was largely hollow, but that did not mean that Charles might not revive its power at the expense of the papacy. To prevent this, Leo openly supported Francis and privately pushed Henry, hoping that the three-way race might result in a deadlock and the electors would then compromise on some petty German prince who would trouble no one.

The accepted method of campaigning was to shower the electors with money. Both Charles and Francis were lavish with bribes, but Henry was uncharacteristically frugal. His agent was instructed to make promises, but pay only after he was chosen.

For the electors, a bribe in hand was worth two in the bush. Besides, even though Charles had grown up in the Netherlands and was as foreign to the German states as Francis or Henry, he was at least Maximilian's grandson. On June 28, 1519, Henry's twenty-eighth birthday, the electors named Charles Holy Roman Emperor. As Charles V he ruled the Netherlands, Spain, part of Italy, the German states, and Austria. In addition Columbus and other explorers sailing under the Spanish flag had discovered new lands across the sea, which made Charles ruler of much of the New World.

The fate of Europe was now in the hands of three young monarchs. Charles was nineteen, Francis was twenty-five, and Henry was twenty-eight. As rivals Charles and Francis were fairly well matched. Charles had more square miles of real estate, but his possessions were scattered, and his sixteen million European subjects were too diversified to unite easily if at all. Francis ruled a compact land mass with fourteen million subjects. His domain

47

was smaller than Charles's, but it was strategically located.

Thus Henry held the key to mastery of Europe. If he allied himself with Charles, Francis might be crushed. If he allied himself with Francis, they could close every route between Charles's northern and southern possessions. If he kept the peace, they might keep the peace as well.

Both kings immediately began to court Henry. Francis suggested that the proposed meeting, which had been postponed by the Imperial election, be held as soon as possible. He and Henry could "give laws to Christendom," he said.

But Charles knew the value of Henry's friendship too, and he had a powerful friend at court. Henry's wife, Catherine of Aragon, was Charles's aunt; he was the son of her sister, Joanna the Mad.

Catherine advised Charles to stop in England to see Henry before his meeting with Francis. Wolsey was cool to this plan because he favored an English-French alliance. There was no room in his schemes for Charles, since he believed England and France needed each other's support against the emperor's potentially overwhelming strength. Besides, he was getting pensions from France that he didn't want to endanger.

Wolsey proceeded with plans for Henry and Francis to meet near Calais in the summer of 1520. Meanwhile Catherine urged the emperor to hasten to England before Henry departed. The jostling between Catherine and Wolsey over Charles and Francis was well known, and the French ambassador grew concerned. One day he suggested that perhaps Henry did not really want to meet the king of France. Henry swore that he did indeed, and to prove it, he would not shave again until they embraced.

Reddish whiskers soon sprouted on the royal jowls as a token of Henry's promise. After a few months there was a problem with the arrangements and Henry shaved. The French feared that Catherine had won and the meeting would be cancelled. But in a week the beard was sprouting again and the French diplomats sighed with relief. Every morning they watched the king's chin for a sign of whether or not the meeting with Francis would be held.

Charles managed to reach England just as Henry was preparing to embark for France. Henry rode down to Dover to greet him, and then they rode to Canterbury for three days of banquets and discussions. No one knew exactly what was said, for even Wolsey was excluded from their meetings. But Henry was well pleased. For the first time in history, a Holy Roman Emperor had visited England, and he came in the form of a youth, Henry's nephew, humbly seeking advice from his older and wiser uncle. Charles, who was far shrewder than Henry knew, cemented the relationship by later writing to thank the English king for "the advice you gave me like a good father when we were at Cantorberi."

After seeing Charles, Henry sailed for Calais. The place chosen for his meeting with Francis was a valley near Calais, which came to be called the Field of Cloth of Gold. Wolsey was in charge of all the arrangements, and because the cardinal could not do anything modestly, the meeting was one of the great spectacles of the age.

Wolsey had thousands of laborers build tents and pavilions for the English, as well as an instant palace for feasting and entertainment. Attached to the palace was a chapel with thirty-five priests and a boys' choir. For himself Wolsey had a private chapel prefabricated in England and shipped to France to be erected at the site.

Wolsey would spare no detail to make this peaceful invasion of France as impressive as the real invasion had been seven years earlier. Henry and Catherine sailed with some six thousand attendants and thirty-two hundred horses. The English even brought their own food, including over two thousand sheep and four bushels of mustard.

On June 7, Henry and Francis met at a carefully prearranged spot on the Field of Cloth of Gold. They embraced warmly. Spectators noticed that the French king was taller but the English king was handsomer.

The two monarchs, their queens, and their vast entourages entertained each other spectacularly. Each tried to surpass the other in lavishness and in demonstrating his skill at the table, in the jousts, or in the dance. One day Henry felt boisterous after beating Francis at archery. He playfully seized Francis' collar and said, "Come, you shall wrestle with me." Francis was so agreeable that in a moment he had Henry flat on his royal back.

When Henry rose he was no longer playful. "Again!" he snarled. But both queens and a group of courtiers tactfully came between the two kings with light, irrelevant chatter, and smoothed the moment over.

On June 24, Henry and Francis exchanged their final gifts and vows and parted. "These sovereigns," wrote a contemporary, "are not at peace. They adapt themselves to circumstances, but they hate each other very cordially." As the English rode from the field, one noble was heard to say, "By God, when I meet those Frenchmen again I hope it may be with my sword point!"

If the English had to choose either Charles or Francis for an ally, they would take Charles for several reasons. Their hatred of the French was rooted in the Hundred Years' War. Charles was the nephew of their Queen Catherine, who was much loved in England. Finally, Charles ruled the Netherlands, which was the chief market for English wool and cloth. War with Charles would be disastrous for trade; war with France would satisfy an ancient longing.

Henry shared the English attitude. From the Field of Cloth of Gold he rode directly to a second meeting with the Emperor Charles. They agreed that Henry should go no further in his negotiations to wed his young daughter to Francis' son. And they agreed that Charles would go no further with his plan to wed Francis' daughter. Instead they discussed the possibility of four-year-old Mary Tudor marrying the Holy Roman Emperor. The son of Charles and Mary would be heir to England, Spain, the empire, and the lands across the sea. Henry might not be father of a king but, even better, he might be grandfather of the emperor of the world.

# 5 ⟿ Death and Taxes

IN ORDER to have something to pass on to his heirs, however, Henry had to hold on to what he had. Like his father he was always alert to any sign that someone coveted the throne, especially since he had no son and the succession might be disputed. In the spring of 1521, the duke of Buckingham, who was the nearest male heir to the throne, was accused of boasting that he would be king if Henry died without a son.

The testimony came from Buckingham's servants, but there was some suspicion they had been bribed or tortured by Cardinal Wolsey, for the blueblood and the butcher's boy hated each other. One day Buckingham had held a basin of water for the king to wash his hands. When the king was done, Wolsey had dipped his own common hands in the basin. The duke was so outraged that he emptied the basin over Wolsey's feet. The incident was remembered when Buckingham was beheaded for treason in May, and some said flatly that Wolsey had exploited Henry's sensitivity about the lack of a son to get rid of an enemy at court. "The butcher's dog has pulled down the fairest buck in Christendom," commented Charles V.

For Henry the axe was a decisive way to deal with unruly subjects, but unruly foreigners were more of a problem. One of them was Martin Luther. In 1517 Luther, an obscure German friar, had nailed a paper to the church door at Wittenberg which questioned the sale of indulgences, or pardons. The church was so badly in need of reform that Luther's criticism caught fire. In 1520 he published a book, *The Babylonian Captivity of the Church*, in which he went further and denied the supremacy of the pope, criticized the mass, and accepted only three of the seven sacraments. Luther was excommunicated from the church, but his heresy flamed through Europe, particularly in Scandinavia and the German states.

Rome asked Henry to do what he could to damp down the heretical fires, and Wolsey suggested the king attack the problem in a manner befitting a learned Renaissance prince. Henry would write a book to counter the Lutheran arguments, and write it he did, with the aid of a team of ghosts including Thomas More, who was considered by Erasmus to be England's one genius. "All the learned men in England have taken part in its composition," commented one ambassador. The book was called *The Defense of the Seven Sacraments* and it was to embarrass its author later since it stoutly supported the papacy, attacked schism and heresy, and defended the sacraments, particularly marriage.

The pope was pleased with Henry's work, and the king looked to Rome for a reward. Charles was called "His Catholic Majesty." Francis was "Most Christian King." Henry wanted a papal title too. So Pope Leo proclaimed him "Defender of the

Faith," which led the king's fool to say, "Prithee, good Harry, let thee and I defend one another and leave the faith alone to defend itself."

While Henry sought praise and honor from the pope, Wolsey went a step further and sought the papacy itself. Henry encouraged Wolsey's ambition, and both Francis and Charles exploited it by promising to deliver votes to him at the next papal election. Wolsey made his first lunge at the papacy when Leo X died in December, 1521. The college of cardinals was deadlocked for fourteen days, but Wolsey got votes on only one ballot, and then only seven.

The new pope, Adrian VI, announced that he intended to clean out corruption in Rome, and he made enough of a start to lead the Venetian ambassador in the Holy City to write, "All Rome is horrified at what the pope has accomplished in one short week."

But Adrian lived less than two years. In 1523 there was another papal election. Wolsey pressured both Henry and Charles for support, but although it took fifty days to choose a new pope, Wolsey did not get a single vote. The cardinals' choice was an Italian, Giulio de' Medici, who became Clement VII.

If Wolsey could not rule the world from Rome, he would do what he could from London. As always there was work for his busy hands. The perpetual peace he had arranged with considerable pomp in 1518 had gone the way of all perpetual peaces. Francis was trying to provoke Charles in Navarre and in Italy in order to get the emperor to attack him for, by the Treaty of London, England was bound to go to war against the aggressor. Soon both emperor and king were accusing each other of aggression and demanding Henry's support.

Henry's sympathies were with Charles, but he needed more time to prepare for war. In the summer of 1521, he sent Wolsey to Calais. Publicly the cardinal was to mediate between Francis and Charles; privately he was to make an alliance with Charles for a joint attack on Francis. At Calais, Wolsey went though the charade of acting as mediator, then he went off to see the emperor. Charles agreed to join Henry in an invasion of France in the spring of 1523. He also agreed to marry Mary Tudor.

Sixteenth-century wars, like wars at any other time, cost money, and a year before the proposed campaign of 1523, Wolsey faced the disagreeable business of raising funds to pay for arms, ships, and provisions. First he demanded a loan from the London merchants and then he tried a property tax, but the complaints were so bitter that Wolsey decided Parliament would have to be summoned.

The Parliament that met in April, 1523, was the first in eight years, and the only one called while Wolsey ruled England. Wolsey asked the members for a huge sum to pay for the next war with France. After one hundred days of bickering and threats, the money was finally raised, but not without some angry scenes between Wolsey and the Commons, and bitter grumbling throughout the country against the cardinal, wherever the tax collectors came.

The English did not want more war, but Henry did, very badly. He was so impatient for action that he had already sent a small army to France in the summer of 1522. All the men did was burn harmless villages and complain, as always, about the lack of beer. The commander wrote Wolsey, "There is universal poverty here, and great fear of this army. I trust the king's grace and you will be content with our services."

The war began in earnest the following summer. The duke of Suffolk set out with a large army to invade France from Calais, in the north. Charles would attack from the south. The duke of Bourbon, a French noble who had risen against his king, would attack from the east.

Suffolk pushed to within fifty miles of Paris, but by then it was November. Dispirited by bad weather and news that the troops of Charles and Bourbon had been turned back, the English demanded to go home, and home they went.

It was the campaign of 1512 all over again. Henry had been humiliated once more, and another costly war had gained neither an inch of territory nor a bit of booty. Henry blustered about another invasion, but by the beginning of 1524, Wolsey was negotiating secretly with the French for a separate peace. The cardinal had always preferred Francis to Charles, particularly since he felt that the emperor had betrayed his promises to make him pope.

But the war was not over yet. By the fall of 1524, Francis had repulsed all of his invaders and decided to do some invading of his own. He led his army into Italy to recapture the duchy of Milan, which he had lost to Charles. The main Imperialist force was at Pavia, twenty-two miles south of Milan. Francis lost thirty-five hundred men in one day, trying to storm Pavia, but he failed to take the city. Refusing to retreat, he decided on a siege.

Siege was a common enough tactic, but not in winter. The French troops suffered wretchedly from exposure. "The infantry lie in the trenches and dare not leave them, lest they should die of hunger and cold," wrote an observer.

While Francis was warming himself in his kitchen at Pavia, the duke of Bourbon reorganized his forces and marched to the relief of the city. Bourbon's army attacked the French at midnight on February 23, 1525. As Bourbon struck from one side, the troops in Pavia rode out of the city and attacked from the other. Francis' army was slaughtered in between.

Unlike Henry, Francis fought his own battles. He was lying on the ground, wounded, when an Imperialist soldier pressed a sword to his side and ordered him to surrender. "Give me my life," said Francis, "for I am the king. I yield myself up to the emperor."

The battle of Pavia was fought on Charles's birthday. On the day the emperor became twenty-five years old, his troops gave him as a present the king of France for his prisoner.

Solemn Charles would not celebrate his enemy's ignominious defeat, but Henry knew no such restraint. When the news was brought to his bedchamber on the morning of March 9, he forgot he was in the process of making peace with France. He remembered only that he hated Francis, that Charles was his nephew, and that France was now without a king. "You are as welcome as the angel Gabriel was to the Virgin Mary," he gloatingly told the messenger.

Henry's first thought was to profit from Francis' defeat. "Now is the time," he said, "for the emperor and myself to devise the means of getting full satisfaction from France. Not an hour is to be lost."

Henry wanted nothing less than to seize Francis' vacant throne. Charles could have some French territory, and Bourbon would also get a share, but the crown was to be for Henry. Of course it would pass to Charles eventually, as the husband of Henry's sole heir.

With this in mind, Henry tried to get Charles to agree to

what he hoped would be the death blow to the French royal family. He did not think France could resist a joint invasion now, with its king in captivity and the queen-mother, Louise of Savoy, ruling as regent. But Charles would not cooperate. Like his grandfather Maximilian, he was always in debt. He felt that Henry "should make the rest of any conquest at his own charge." Charles could get what he wanted from Francis because the French king was his prisoner. He was not going to spend money and arms in order to swell the power of England.

Besides, he had other things to worry about. Luther's teachings had so inflamed the German peasants with ideas of greater freedom and defiance of authority that they were revolting against the nobility. It was the greatest mass uprising in German history and, ironically, Luther opposed it. He told the nobles to kill the peasants "like mad dogs," which they very willingly did.

But with or without Charles's help, Henry was determined to take the French throne. At this point the king did not have much more money than the emperor, having exhausted his purse in repeated and futile adventures on the continent. But if he didn't have any money, he had a lord chancellor who could bleed a stone. Henry turned to Wolsey to raise funds for yet another invasion of France.

This time Wolsey would not summon Parliament, for two years earlier the members had made too much fuss and had taken too long. Funds had to be found quickly and quietly, so the king's advisers decided it would be best to go directly to the people. They left the details to Wolsey.

Wolsey tried what was called the Amicable Grant. It was

neither a grant, nor was it amicable. It was a tax and it had to be paid. "Resist not," the cardinal bluntly warned a group of London merchants, "otherwise it may fortune to cost some their heads."

But even so dire a threat had little effect. This time the people did more than grumble; they refused to pay. Henry had squandered his father's fortune, plus all the heavy taxes and loans granted him, and he had nothing to show for it but more debts.

The tax collectors met opposition everywhere, and there was some open rebellion. When the duke of Norfolk asked a group of armed resisters who their captain was, one of them replied, "His name is Poverty, for he and his cousin Necessity have brought us to this doing."

Since the people were reluctant to speak ill of the king, the symbol of their nation, they vented their anger on Wolsey. "All people cursed the cardinal," wrote Hall. The cardinal kept lowering his demands, but resistance won. No tyrant can counter the will of a united and determined opposition. Before long the absolute monarch of England was claiming that he "never knew" about the grant. His absolute minister said it wasn't his idea and he had never agreed to it.

Henry lusted so painfully for the French crown that when he failed to raise money at home he tried to borrow it abroad for this invasion that interested no one but himself. He even asked Charles for funds, but the English agents reported that there was no point in blowing "at a dead coal."

Charles not only had no money, but he was deeply in debt to his future father-in-law. The emperor needed money so badly that while Henry was trying to get some from him, he was trying to get some in turn by asking Henry to send the Princess Mary and her dowry to Spain at once.

Henry refused and Charles broke the marriage contract. As Holy Roman Emperor he felt he could raise a better price than Henry offered. He married his cousin, Isabella of Portugal, who brought him three times Mary's dowry, and there were no debts due on it.

Charles's rebuff cut more deeply than any other humiliation Henry had suffered. His daughter would not be empress; his grandson would not rule the Christian world. For Henry's infantile politics and emotions, there was only one predictable response. He decided to avenge the insult by making an alliance against Charles and with France, the very nation he had been prepared to vanquish just a few months earlier.

The new Anglo-French treaty was ready by the end of August, 1525. It provided, among other things, that Mary would wed one of Francis' sons. A few months later, in January, 1526, Charles released the French king. After ten months in captivity, Francis was amenable to almost anything. Since his first wife was dead, he agreed to marry Charles's sister. "I'd marry Charles's mule, if necessary," he said. The king also agreed to surrender to Charles large portions of territory in both France and Italy, but this was a promise he never intended to keep. He disavowed it as soon as he was released.

When Francis was free again, he joined a new alliance with the Italian states, including the papacy, against Charles. Fighting promptly broke out in Italy, where the emperor had a large concentration of men.

By the spring of 1527, an Imperial army under the command of the duke of Bourbon was marching on Rome. It was a particularly vicious group, for the men were mercenaries—soldiers who fought for pay—and they had not been paid. They were hungry, and Rome had wealth beyond their dreams. They were soldiers of the emperor, and Rome was their enemy. The Germans among them were Lutheran, and to them, the pope represented not Christ but antichrist.

Swelled by throngs of Italian peasants looking for booty, this angry army attacked Rome on May 6. Bourbon was slain in the first assault, which left the men not only undisciplined but leaderless. By afternoon they had entered the city, murdering and looting at will. The pope fled from the Vatican to the Castle of St. Angelo, where he was, for all practical purposes, a prisoner of Charles V, the Holy Roman Emperor.

It took three weeks for news of the sack of Rome to reach England. According to the chronicler Hall, ordinary men cared very little about the fate of Clement VII, remarking that, "the pope was a ruffian, unworthy of his place, that he began the mischief, and that he was well served." But Henry and Wolsey cared a great deal. For Henry needed the pope's help in a delicate personal matter, an annulment. The pope was now a prisoner of Charles V, and Charles V was the nephew of the woman Henry wanted to be rid of.

# 6 ❧ Princes Do Not Marry for Love

"PRINCES do not marry for love," a diplomat once said, "they take wives only to beget children." Yet Henry had married Catherine for love. At least, in the early years of his marriage he sought her advice, kept her at his side at feasts and entertainments, and wore her initials on his sleeve when he fought in jousts and tournaments.

In return Catherine was a kind and loving wife, but she could not give her husband what he wanted most—a son. Although she suffered many pregnancies, the only child who survived was the girl, Mary.

Catherine had come to England in 1501 as a slim, pretty teen-ager. She was still pretty when she married Henry, even though she was five and one-half years his senior. But repeated pregnancies had thickened her graceful figure and repeated sorrow had aged her beyond her years. The French king remarked brutally, "My brother of England has no son because, although a young and handsome man, he keeps an old and ugly wife."

But Catherine's age and appearance would not alone have

been reason for dissolving the marriage. Henry was no less faithful than any monarch of his age, but he was no more faithful either. Even in the years when he still cared about his wife, he had his mistresses as well. This was so commonplace for a king that it did not trouble Catherine, as long as her position as queen was not jeopardized.

But while she bore dead children, the king was more fortunate with at least one of his mistresses. In 1519, a lady-in-waiting named Elizabeth Blount gave birth to a son. Henry acknowledged the boy as his and named him Henry Fitzroy, the ancient French term for "son of a king."

Bessie Blount was married off and the boy was kept out of sight. But in 1525, when Charles roiled Henry by breaking his agreement to marry Mary, six-year-old Henry Fitzroy was led before the court, given a host of honors and titles, and made first peer of England. Having lost the possibility of having the emperor as his son-in-law, it seemed that Henry might put Mary aside and make his illegitimate son his legitimate heir. But at the end of the year, Henry sent Mary to the Welsh border to take up the duties of princess of Wales, the title traditionally accorded the heir to the throne.

If Henry was in doubt about the succession to the throne, he had reason. He had a legitimate daughter, but the only woman who had ever tried to claim the throne of England had led it to a disastrous civil war. He had an illegitimate son, but if he tried to make him his heir there would be rival claims for Mary and others with legitimate royal blood. This too might lead to civil war.

Henry VIII had no way of reading the future; he knew only the past. He knew too well the story of the Wars of the Roses.

He knew that one of the reasons his father had brought stability to England was because he was able to assure a peaceful succession.

Henry had no way of knowing that not just one, but two of his daughters would rule England. He also overlooked the fact that if female descent was not to be recognized, his own claim was questionable, since it came through his grandmother. But Henry had a way of averting his eyes from the truth when it suited him, and it suited him in this matter.

One way to assure a peaceful succession through his daughter Mary was to marry her to the young king of Scotland, James V. As the son of Henry's older sister, James was already the nearest male heir to the Tudor throne. Together, Mary and James could have ruled England and Scotland, thus resolving the question of the succession and uniting the neighboring but antagonistic kingdoms.

Henry did not make the Scottish match for Mary. He decided he would produce his own heir. If Catherine could not do it, he knew the woman who would. Her name was Anne Boleyn.

Anne Boleyn came from a long line of social climbers. She was descended from a tradesman who made a fortune and married above him. Each generation of her family seemed to make a better marriage, until the Boleyns became not only wealthy but powerful. Several members of Anne's family served Henry VIII, each in his own way. Both her father Thomas and her brother George were ambassadors. According to rumor, her mother was Henry's first mistress. Anne's older sister Mary was definitely Henry's mistress for a number of years.

In 1519, when Anne was about twelve years old, she was sent to the French court to complete her education. In 1522, when war was pending between England and France, Sir Thomas Boleyn, who was the English ambassador to France, sent his daughter home. Soon after, she came to the English court. Henry apparently noticed her scarcely, if at all.

If Henry paid no attention to her, several other men did. One was Lord Henry Percy, a member of Cardinal Wolsey's household. But Percy was already betrothed, and Anne was to marry an Irish chieftain for political reasons. Henry ordered Wolsey to break up the romance between Anne and Percy.

Wolsey summoned Percy and told him that Anne was not good enough for him. He commanded the youth, in the name of the king, to forget her. Percy obeyed and married as directed. Anne's Irish match never came about, but she was banished from the court. She went off in a pout to the Netherlands and did not return until 1525. This time Henry noticed her.

The secret of Anne Boleyn's fascination for Henry VIII is buried by history. An ambassador wrote that she was "of middling stature, swarthy complexion, long neck, wide mouth, bosom not much raised, and in fact has nothing but the king's great appetite, and her eyes, which are black and beautiful." She also had a deformity on her left hand, a growth that looked like the beginning of a sixth finger.

But even if she was less than beautiful, she contrasted sharply with Catherine of Aragon. Anne was gay and vivacious; Catherine was pious and solemn. Anne was perhaps eighteen; Catherine was thirty-nine. Catherine already belonged to Henry; Anne

65

refused to unless he made her his wife.

When Henry met Anne, her sister had been and perhaps still was his mistress, and he expected the same courtesy from Anne, since women neither resisted nor refused him. But Anne was more ambitious than Mary. Being Henry's mistress had gotten her sister nowhere. Anne wanted more than a pension and a husband when the king was through with her. If she had to endure Henry, whom she did not love, she would make it worth her while. When Henry approached her, she replied demurely, "Your wife I cannot be because you have a queen already. Your mistress I will not be."

Anne's price was the crown itself. It was a daring gamble, but it worked because she had appeared at a unique moment in Henry's life. He was tired of his wife. He was furious with the Spanish alliance, which she represented. He wanted a son. A new marriage and a new queen would solve his problems.

In the normal course of events, Henry's annulment should have been a routine matter. Popes usually granted annulments as needed to persons of influence, including members of Henry's own family. Henry's friend, the duke of Suffolk, had two previous marriages annulled after he wed Henry's sister Mary. Henry's other sister, Margaret, and her lover had earlier marriages annulled so they could marry each other.

Almost anyone of importance could get an annulment for a fee and a reason, and the reason did not have to be as good as the fee. But Henry had a reason; his wife was his brother's widow. The Bible (Leviticus, XX : 21) says: "If a man shall take his brother's wife, it is an impurity: . . . they shall be childless." After eighteen years of marriage, Henry decided that marrying his brother's widow had been a sin. God had punished him by making him childless, or as good as childless, since only a daughter survived.

Henry had needed a dispensation to marry Arthur's widow, but he had gotten one, for such marriages were made and such dispensations were given. Besides, if there was one text in the Bible that seemed to forbid such a marriage, there was another that seemed to mandate it. Deuteronomy (XXV : 5) says: "When brethren dwell together, and one of them dieth without children, the wife of the deceased shall not marry to another; but his brother shall take her, and raise up seed for his brother."

Henry was not unaware that he had married his brother's widow and that he had needed a papal dispensation to do so. At the time of his marriage, he had specifically cited the dispensation when he wrote, "we could not, without offense to God, right, reason, and good conscience, do otherwise than as we have done." He had known all along about the prohibition in Leviticus, but his conscience did not reverse itself until he met Anne Boleyn. In Shakespeare's *Henry VIII*, a chamberlain says to the duke of Norfolk, "It seems the marriage with his brother's wife / Has crept too near his conscience." And the duke of Suffolk remarks as an aside, "No, his conscience / Has crept too near another lady."

In 1527, having finally noticed that he had been living with his brother's widow for almost two decades, Henry decided to have the marriage annulled. To do this, he wanted the bull of Pope Julius II, which had permitted him to wed Catherine, declared invalid. If this were done, then the marriage itself would also be invalid. Thus he initiated his attempt to assure a peaceful succession to the throne with a move which would result in his only legitimate child being made illegitimate.

Henry began the process of getting an annulment in the spring of 1527. It was to be done simply and quickly. Cardinal Wolsey, as papal legate, would declare Julius II's dispensation invalid, and the marriage would automatically be annulled. This would be confirmed in Rome.

Wolsey was only too happy to accommodate the king. He did not like Catherine or her nephew, the emperor, and he wanted Henry free to wed a French princess and seal the new Anglo-French alliance. Therefore, on May 17, Wolsey summoned Henry to a court at the cardinal's residence at Westminster to answer charges that he had been unlawfully living with his brother's widow for the last eighteen years. The judges were Wolsey and William Warham, the archbishop of Canterbury. Their court was a sham not only because it was called at the king's request and to serve his purpose but also because it was held secretly so Catherine could not appear to defend her marriage.

The court met several times in May to hear Henry's lawyer argue against the papal dispensation. It was still in session when word reached England that Imperialist troops had sacked Rome. Wolsey was disconsolate. "If the pope be slain or taken," he wrote, "it will hinder the king's affairs not a little, which have hitherto been going so well."

When it was clear that the pope was Charles's prisoner, Wolsey revised his plans. He adjourned the court without a verdict and prepared to go to France to seek aid to free the pope or, failing that, to rule in his place.

Meanwhile, Catherine had to be told what was happening. It took Henry less time to decide to go to war than it did to find the courage to face his wife. She knew about the trial at Westminster; there were too many loose tongues at court to keep such a secret. Therefore she was not surprised when Henry finally told her they had been living in sin for eighteen years. She was not surprised, but she was outraged and she wept.

Henry could deal with ambassadors and emperors and kings, but he could not deal with women. He could not handle Anne Boleyn, who wanted his crown, and he could not handle Catherine, who wanted her honor. Catherine could overlook the king's mistresses, but annulment was something else. It was an admission that this pious woman had been unlawfully married. It also meant that her daughter would be declared illegitimate and barred from the throne.

Henry might doubt their marriage, but Catherine did not. She felt that the text in Leviticus did not apply to them because she had been Arthur's wife in name only. She knew, and Henry knew, that Arthur had never consummated his marriage. She was Henry's wife and England's queen and she would never say otherwise.

Her words and her tears unnerved Henry. He mumbled something about everything turning out alright, asked her not to tell anyone what he had told her, and fled from her room.

His plea for secrecy came too late, for by then all London knew of what was called the king's "great matter." "The affair is as notorious as if it had been proclaimed by the town crier," wrote the Imperial ambassador. From the beginning of Henry's attempt to win an annulment, most of the people sided with their queen. "They cannot believe that [the king] will ever carry so wicked a project into effect," the ambassador said. Catherine may have come to them from Spain, but the English loved her better than their Henry. They knew her for her wisdom, her piety, and her charity. They also resented the fact that Princess Mary would be made illegitimate. If Henry was really concerned about whether the people would accept Mary as his successor, he had his answer in their opposition to the annulment. But Henry was not seeking that kind of evidence; he was looking for justification to marry Anne Boleyn.

Catherine decided to fight the annulment, but she knew that with the king the almighty power in England, she would get little help from anyone who mattered. The only place she could turn to was Spain and the only significant person who might help her was her nephew Charles. In mid-July, a messenger sped from Catherine to the emperor. Henry ordered him intercepted, but somehow he evaded all pursuers and brought Catherine's plea to Charles. She begged her nephew to use his influence with the pope to have the case tried in Rome and to have Wolsey's commission as papal legate revoked. Charles replied, "You may be certain that nothing shall be omitted on my part to help you. . . ."

Thus the battle was joined. Because the pope was Charles's prisoner, what should have been an ordinary royal annulment, routinely processed by Rome, became a searing issue that forever altered the history of both the church and England.

But schism was still in the future when Cardinal Wolsey sailed to France in the summer of 1527 with his immodest plan to free the pope or assume his power. He was not only thoroughly unsuccessful, but while he was abroad he was alarmed to learn that Henry was busy behind his back. Without consulting or informing the cardinal, the king had decided to send his secretary, William Knight, to Rome. Knight was to ask Clement to give Henry permission to marry Anne, if the annulment of the first marriage were granted.

For Henry's case had an indelicate irony. In matters of affinity, canon, or church, law did not distinguish between licit and illicit unions. Catherine had been the wife of Henry's brother, but Anne was the sister of Henry's mistress. According to canon law Anne was related to Henry in the same degree of affinity that he was related to Catherine. If he was forbidden to marry Catherine, he was also forbidden to marry Anne.

Thus at the same time Henry was arguing that Pope Julius had no right to issue a dispensation that allowed him to marry his brother's widow, he was asking Pope Clement to issue a dispensation to allow him to marry his mistress' sister.

Wolsey was appalled when he learned about Knight's mission, even though he did not know all the details, for it clearly signified that the king was making his own moves and the cardinal was no longer indispensable. As soon as possible, Wolsey hurried home to reassess and reassert his power. When he reached Richmond Palace, he sent word to Henry to ask where he wished to see him, since it was customary for the king to speak to him privately when important matters had to be discussed.

The cardinal's messenger found the king with Anne Boleyn. Before Henry could reply to Wolsey's question, Anne snapped,

"Where else should the cardinal come? Tell him he may come here, where the king is."

Wolsey obediently went to the room and saw Anne Boleyn seated at the king's side. If he had not known it sooner, he suddenly realized who now ruled the ruler of England.

*Illustrations*

*Henry VIII*
*at about twenty years of age*

*Catherine of Aragon, the Spanish princess*
*who was Henry's first wife*

Myne — Awne good Cardinall I recomande me vnto yow
w all my hart and thankes yow for the grette payne
and laboure that yow do take in my bysynes and maters
deszyryng yow (that wen yow have well establysshyd them)
to take sume pastyme and cofort to the intente yow may
the lenger enduze to serve vs for allweys payne can not
be induryd / surly yow have so substancyally orderyd owr
maters bothe off thys syde the see and by onde that in my
oppynyon lytyll or nothyng can be addyd / neuertheless accordyng
to your desyze I do send yow myne oppynyon by thys bearar
the refformacion wherof I do remytte to yow and the
remnante off our trusty coselleers wych I am sure that
substantially lokes on hyt / as tochyng the mater that sr
wylliam styns broght answear off I am well cotentyd
w what order so ever yow do take in att the quene
my wyff hathe desyryd me to make haz most harty
recommendatyons to yow as to hym that she louuys
very well and bothe she and I wolde knowe fayne
wen yow wyll repayre to vs / no more to yow
att thys tyme but that w godys helpe I trust we shall
desapoynte owr onymys off theyre intendyd porpose
wryttyn w the hand of your louyng master

H REX

*Left, a letter written by Henry to Cardinal Wolsey, right, one of the most powerful figures in Henry's court*

*A bas-relief of Henry arriving at the Field of Cloth of Gold*

ANNA BOLINA VXOR- ... IENRI· OCTA

*Left, the ship* Henry Grace-à-Dieu,
*which was built for Henry in 1512. It
was said of Anne Boleyn, above, that
she "in fact has nothing but . . . her
eyes, which are black and beautiful"*

*Above, Sir Thomas More, painted by
Hans Holbein. Right, Thomas Cromwell,
who, like two of Henry's wives, was executed*

*Below, Sir Thomas Cranmer, who was warned by the king of a plot against him. Right, Jane Seymour, the mother of Edward, Henry's only legitimate son*

Henry said about Anne of Cleves, Above:
"I like her not." Right, Henry, in the
rich clothes and jewels he enjoyed

·ETATIS·       SVÆ·21

*Left, Catherine Howard, the fifth wife
of Henry VIII. Above, Henry's last
wife, Catherine Parr.*

*The title page of the Bible in English.*

# 7 ❧ All or None

WOLSEY had planned to wed his king to a French princess; Henry had chosen an English lady-in-waiting. Instead of making a brilliant diplomatic match, the king would bring to power a woman who despised the cardinal for breaking up her romance with Henry Percy and who had immediately become the leader of Wolsey's many enemies at court.

Yet whatever Wolsey's private feelings about Anne Boleyn may have been, he still continued earnestly to try to procure the annulment. He may have hoped that by the time he got it, Anne would have been dropped for someone else, for like the rest of the court, Wolsey believed Anne was Henry's mistress and the infatuation would not hold. What Wolsey did not know was that Anne held power over Henry not because she was his mistress, but because she was not.

Catherine of Aragon, who had seen Henry's women come and go, appeared to understand that this one would not go quietly. Since Anne was one of her ladies-in-waiting, the rivals saw each other at court. One day they played cards, and Anne was lucky with her kings. Said Catherine wryly, "You have good hap to stop at a king, my lady Anne, but you are not like others, you will have all or none."

Anne's chances of having all were high, because Henry mooned over his unconquered conquest. When she was away he wrote her lovesick letters. "I beseech you earnestly," said one, "to let me know your real mind as to the love between us two. It is needful for me to obtain this answer of you, having been for a whole year wounded with the dart of love, and not yet assured whether I shall succeed in finding a place in your heart and affection."

Since the acquisition of the annulment was dragging on, Henry repeated his original offer. "If you please to do the duty of a true and loyal mistress," he wrote, "and to give up yourself, heart and person, to me, who will be, as I have been, your most loyal servant . . . I promise you that . . . I will take you for my mistress, casting off all others that are in competition with you out of my thoughts and affections, and serving you only."

The king begged and the king was refused. Henry was no prize; the crown was. Anne coyly told him, "I will rather lose my life than my virtue, which will be the greatest and best part of the dowry I shall bring to my husband." Having had so little experience with virtue, Henry accepted Anne's as genuine.

The key to the annulment rested with the pope, and the key to the pope literally rested with the Emperor Charles, who was his captor. But having the pope in captivity was as embarrassing for Charles as it was inconvenient for Henry, so the emperor agreed to let Clement escape. Disguised in a peasant's blouse and a false beard, his Holiness passed through the gates of the Castle of St. Angelo and rode in a cart to the town of Orvieto, where he took refuge in the palace of the local bishop.

William Knight, the messenger Henry had sent without consulting Wolsey, had not been able to see Clement in Rome, so he followed the pope to Orvieto to present Henry's case. But Clement knew his freedom was an illusion; he was still very much at the mercy of the emperor. He also knew that Henry had a debatable argument in asking one pope to undo a dispensation that another pope had every right to issue. Finally, Clement was cautious and indecisive by nature. Very early in the question of the king's great matter, he seems to have concluded that the best course would be to hasten slowly. He did not want to antagonize either the king or the emperor. Therefore it seemed wise always to seem to be doing something, while carefully undoing it at the same time, so that in the end, nothing was achieved. In this way he might delay long enough for the king to lose interest in his new love, or for Catherine to die a natural death, and the matter would be resolved.

Thus Clement saw Knight and gave him a dispensation for Henry to marry Anne, if the first marriage was proved to be unlawful. But he did nothing about invalidating the first marriage.

Not trusting Knight, Wolsey had sent a second emissary to see the pope, an Italian diplomat named Gregory Casale. Casale was to persuade Clement to send a legate to England to try the king's case. The pope was also asked to set up the court in such a way that Henry had to win. With Casale, Clement managed a second standoff by permitting the case to be tried in England but without the specific directions that would make the outcome certain and without promising that Rome would confirm the decision. As far as Clement was concerned, Wolsey already had enough power to try the case and find for Henry. The king could then remarry, and only if the second marriage were challenged would the pope have to be consulted.

But a doubtful second marriage would not satisfy the king's tender conscience. Both Henry and Wolsey wanted the matter settled in advance, and they wanted it settled their way. So early in February, 1528, two more emissaries set out for Orvieto, Edward Fox, the king's almoner, and Stephen Gardiner, Wolsey's secretary.

Day after day, sometimes from seven in the morning until one the following morning, the two men pleaded, argued, and threatened, while the pope sighed and wept. At one point Clement commented that although there was a saying "that the pope had all laws locked up in a cabinet in his heart, yet God never gave him the key to open it."

The more Clement wiped his eyes, the harder Henry's agents pressed him. Finally Clement authorized Wolsey and another papal legate to hear the case. Either one could pronounce sentence if the other chose not to, and the decision would be final; there could be no appeal to Rome. But the papal commission was not as tightly worded as Wolsey wished; it would still be possible for the pope to recall the case before a verdict was reached.

The second legate chosen to weigh the evidence with Wolsey was Cardinal Lorenzo Campeggio, an experienced lawyer and diplomat who had been to London ten years earlier, when another pope was seeking to raise a crusade against the Turks. Campeggio was privately instructed by the pope to try to reconcile Henry and Catherine, or to find some sort of solution, but not to take any important action without consulting Rome. Above all he was to delay as long as possible, because much depended on the outcome of the latest installment of the war in Italy between Charles and Francis.

England had also declared war on the emperor, in January, 1528. "Wolsey is playing a terrible game," wrote the French ambassador, "for I believe he is the only Englishman that wishes a war with Flanders." The ambassador was right. Just the threat of war with England's best market, the Netherlands, was so ruinous to commerce that the country almost rebelled, and a truce was arranged even before the fighting began.

Cardinal Campeggio set out from Rome to London in the summer of 1528, at a pace that would shame a snail. In bad weather the journey might have taken six weeks. Traveling in good weather, Campeggio managed to make it last more than three months. True, the legate was so crippled with gout that his hands could not always hold the reins of his mule and he had to be carried part of the way in a litter. But it was also true that he was keeping his ears open for word of the progress of the war that was raging in Italy.

While Henry was impatiently waiting for Campeggio to reach London, there was another outbreak of the sweating sickness. At the first sign of the epidemic, Henry fled. Every few days he moved to a different palace, farther and farther from London. Although it was summer, he sat for hours before a roaring fire because he thought it would keep the disease at bay. He also went to mass three times a day and revised his will.

Among those Henry left behind when he fled from London was his beloved Anne Boleyn, who fell victim to the sweat. He would shake the church by the roots to make her his wife, but he would not come near her when she was ill. Instead he sent her his second-best doctor and a comforting letter saying that few women ever died of the disease. He was right; Anne Boleyn lived.

Campeggio finally reached London on October 9. His measured pace proved justified, for in the course of his protracted journey the situation in Italy had drastically changed. When Campeggio set out, the French position had looked promising, but after the summer's campaign Charles was once more in charge. The pope's decision would again be made in the shadow of the Holy Roman Emperor.

The legate knew he would not be able to grant the annulment. The emperor opposed it and so must the pope. Campeggio soon learned that many of the English opposed it also. He found his route lined with thousands of women shouting, "No Nan Boleyn for us!"

But two men were determined to have that annulment. Wolsey told Campeggio bluntly that if the king did not get what he wanted, "total ruin would specially ensue of the kingdom, of himself, of the church's influence." Campeggio begged Wolsey to try to reconcile the king and queen but the legate wrote Rome, "I have no more success in persuading the cardinal than if I had spoken to a rock."

He had no better luck with Henry. After seeing the king, Campeggio reported, "His Majesty has studied this case so diligently that I believe he knows more about it than a great theologian or jurist. He told me briefly that he wished nothing except a declaration whether his marriage was valid or not, always presuming it was not, and I think that an angel descending from heaven could not persuade him otherwise."

Campeggio was not about to invalidate the marriage, but he did have a suggestion that appealed to Henry. The matter would be solved if Catherine entered a convent. There was a theological argument that if husband or wife became a religious, he or she underwent a "spiritual death" and the survivor could remarry.

With the king's consent, Campeggio and Wolsey asked Catherine to take the veil. She listened and said little. A few days later she asked Campeggio to hear her confession. In confession she told him that in the four and one-half months of her marriage to Arthur they had spent no more than seven nights together and that the marriage was never consummated. Her marriage to Henry was therefore valid. She also told Campeggio that she "intended to live and die in the estate of matrimony to which God had called her."

Both Campeggio and Wolsey begged her to reconsider, but she refused. The two churchmen had encountered an obstacle rare in their calling; it was called integrity. Henry had bellowed to the world that he and Catherine had lived in sin and that their child was illegitimate. To retire to a nunnery in the face of these assertions would be to acknowledge that they were true, and this Catherine could not in conscience do. She made it clear that even if she were torn "limb from limb," she would fight for the truth, for her rightful place as wife and queen, and for her daughter's rightful claim to the throne.

Campeggio, Wolsey, and Pope Clement himself were aggravated and infuriated by Catherine's decision, because it was inconvenient for them. They had armies, treaties, alliances, and territories to worry about; Catherine was only concerned with the difference between right and wrong. The pope worried about the politics of the annulment; Catherine worried about the morality of it. It was this paradox, rather than the annulment itself, that was to destroy the Catholic Church in England.

While Henry cursed the endless delays that kept him from Anne Boleyn, the people of England cursed also, but for other reasons. They knew why Campeggio had come and their sympathies were wholly with Catherine. Crowds began to cheer her every appearance, and Henry grew concerned. In November, 1528, he summoned a group of notables to share with them the heavy burdens of his conscience.

He began by reminding them how the country had suffered during the Wars of the Roses and how important it was to prevent another civil war by leaving an undisputed succession. Doubts had arisen about his marriage, he explained, and Campeggio had come from Rome to resolve them. "If it may be adjudged by law of God that [Catherine] is my lawful wife," he said, "there was never anything more pleasant and more acceptable to me. . . . If I were to marry again . . . if the marriage might be good, I would surely choose her above all other women."

After speaking further of the doubts concerning his marriage—without admitting that he himself had raised them—Henry said, "These be the pangs that trouble my conscience and for these griefs I seek a remedy." Then he urged everyone to spread the truth, as he had spoken it, about the trial that Campeggio and Wolsey would conduct. If, however, anyone "spoke in any terms than he ought to do of his prince," Henry would show who was master. He was also said to have threatened, according to one account, that "there was never a head so dignified but that he would make it fly."

Henry's hypocrisy fooled no one except himself, for the people knew all about Anne Boleyn, even if he had neglected to mention her. "The people remain quite hardened," wrote the French ambassador, "and I think they would do more if they had more power. . . ." The Imperial ambassador wrote that if six or seven thousand men landed on the English coast to fight for Catherine's cause, they would be joined by forty thousand Englishmen.

By the end of 1528, it was hard to say who was more desperate, Henry or Wolsey. Henry wanted his annulment and Wolsey wanted to keep his position and his head. The pope was now back in Rome, and the cardinal sent no less than five envoys to him to lie, to beg, to threaten, to extort documents to cover every contingency, including one which would permit Henry to have two wives at the same time. Henry also considered offering the pope two thousand soldiers, ostensibly to protect him from the Imperialists, but actually to keep him prisoner until he granted the annulment.

Although Clement was seriously ill, the English agents hounded him ceaselessly, with hints that if Henry did not get what he wanted, he might favor the Lutheran cause. By the spring of 1529, the pope was so openly unsympathetic to him that Henry realized he could make no further progress in Rome. He now decided his best course was to have Campeggio and Wolsey proceed with the trial that had been authorized by Clement the previous year.

The court which was to judge the validity of their marriage commanded the king and queen of England to appear on June 18, 1529, in the Dominican monastery of the Blackfriars. Henry did not attend that day, but Catherine did. She came to object to the trial because the place was hostile and the judges were prejudiced. She also revealed that she had formally requested the pope to try the case in Rome.

When the court met again on June 21, both Henry and Catherine were present. The judges announced they rejected Catherine's objections to the trial. Then Henry spoke. He said he no longer wished to live in sin and asked the legates to decide quickly on the validity of his marriage. Wolsey spoke next and with a straight and solemn face assured everyone he would be a fair and impartial judge.

Then Catherine rose, crossed the courtroom, and knelt at the king's feet. "Sir," she said, "I beseech you for all the love that hath been between us, and for the love of God, let me have justice and right, take of me some pity and compassion, for I am a poor woman and a stranger, born out of your dominion. . . .

"I take God and all the world to witness that I have been to you a true, humble, and obedient wife. . . . This twenty years or more I have been your true wife, and by me ye have had divers children, although it hath pleased God to call them from this world. . . ."

Then, before Henry, before the two cardinal judges, before the notables of the realm who were assembled in the hall, but mostly before God, Catherine made the statement that was the heart of her case. "And when ye had me at the first," she said to Henry, "I take God to be my judge, I was a true maid, without touch of man. And whether this be true or no, I put it to your conscience."

Henry was silent. Then Catherine again challenged the fairness and validity of the trial and asked Henry "to spare me the extremity of this new court. . . . And if ye will not extend to me this favor . . . to God do I commit my cause."

When she was through, Catherine rose, curtseyed to the king, and walked to the door. The crier called out, "Catherine, queen of England, come into the court!" She ignored the order. The crier was commanded to summon her again. "Madame," one of her aides said, "ye be called again."

"It matters not," she replied. "This is no indifferent [impartial] court for me. I will not tarry." And she left.

It was just as well that Catherine did not remain. She was spared the humiliation of hearing the testimony that Henry had dredged out of the dirt of his court to use against his wife. The king did not testify, but bearers of some of the noblest titles in England solemnly paraded as witnesses before the papal court to offer smutty bits of gossip or hearsay about Catherine's first marriage, which had taken place almost thirty years earlier.

In spite of the puerile recollections of aging courtiers, the trial did not go as well as Henry wished. One of Catherine's counsellors was John Fisher, bishop of Rochester. Six feet tall and bare of flesh from fasting and penance, Fisher was the sort of churchman that Henry and Wolsey considered an anomaly, because he cared only for faith and principle.

At one session of the trial, Fisher delivered a stinging defense of the validity of the marriage. At another session the archbishop of Canterbury, William Warham, read a list of bishops who supported Henry's cause, and Fisher's name was among them.

Fisher rose with rage. "That is not my hand nor seal!" he protested. He reminded Warham that when he was asked to sign the document, "I said to you that I would never consent to no such act."

"True," said Warham, "but at the last you were persuaded I should subscribe your name for you, and put a seal to it myself, and you would allow it."

"Under your correction, my lord," said Fisher angrily, "there is no thing more untrue."

Thus Henry's case, packed with perjured, hearsay testimony and forged signatures, moved along. Wolsey tried to push the trial at top speed because Henry hoped that if he presented Clement with a decision in his favor, the pope would accept it, as he had originally agreed to do.

No matter what Wolsey did, the trial did not move fast enough to satisfy Henry. One day he summoned the cardinal, who was supposed to be his judge and had vowed to be an impartial one, and lashed out at him for more than an hour. As the weary Wolsey returned home in his barge, another churchman said to him, "Sir, it is a very hot day." "Yea," said Wolsey bitterly, "and if ye had been as well chafed as I have been within this hour, ye would say it were very hot."

The English agents in Rome were ordered to conceal from the pope the widely known fact that the trial was taking place, but Clement was kept well informed by Campeggio. Once again the pope was seized with a paroxysm of indecision. Should he let the trial proceed to a judgment in Henry's favor or should he bow to the emperor's demand that the case be recalled to Rome? He had little choice; he feared Charles more than Henry.

In mid-July, while the court was still in session at Blackfriars, Clement agreed to recall the case. Henry still hoped for a decision in his favor before the pope's order reached England. But on July 31, Campeggio calmly announced that since this was a Roman court it would follow the Roman calendar and adjourn for a two-month vacation.

Henry's friend and brother-in-law, the duke of Suffolk, exploded in anger. He slammed his fist on a table and said, "Now I see that the old said saw is true, that there was never legate nor cardinal that did good in England."

Wolsey knew these words were meant for him, for he had failed his king. Yet it might have been otherwise. Under the original papal commission, Wolsey had the right to decide the case himself if Campeggio declined. It seemed to Suffolk, as well as to Henry and others, that somehow, at some point, Wolsey could have managed to have the issue resolved in the king's favor. No one knows why he chose not to. Perhaps he still hoped to become pope and did not wish to offend the church. Perhaps he hated or feared Anne Boleyn too much. Or perhaps it was something else.

At that moment in history, the pope was a petty Italian prince rather than the spiritual head of the Roman Catholic Church. But some still saw the ideal rather than the reality. Is there justice and law beyond the state? Henry thought not and he was about to prove it.

But perhaps for Wolsey, as for others, there was, or should have been, a greatness, an order, a justice in Rome that was greater than the work of any king because it belonged to Christ.

Whatever his reasons Wolsey chose church above state, pope above prince, and since he was trapped between the two, the decision had to destroy him.

# 8 ~ Redress, Reformation, and Remedy

WOLSEY failed doubly in the summer of 1529. The papal court was a fiasco and the cardinal's unpopular pro-French policy collapsed. He had allied England with France to check the power of the emperor, but early in August, Francis and Charles signed a treaty making them allies and leaving England isolated. Charles also made peace with Pope Clement, and the pope was even less inclined to offend Charles when he was his ally than when he was his enemy.

Wolsey ruled England solely at the king's pleasure, and the king was no longer pleased. After the summer's disasters, Henry went hunting to spend his anger. Wolsey did not see him again until September 14. When Campeggio went to bid farewell to the king before leaving for Rome, Wolsey was permitted to come along.

To everyone's surprise, the king greeted Wolsey warmly. He took him aside from the staring courtiers and they talked privately for a long time. After dinner, king and cardinal again met privately and talked until nightfall. Then Henry told Wolsey he would see him in the morning.

The cardinal's enemies were dismayed, none more so than Anne Boleyn. As soon as she got Henry's ear she filled it with venomous remarks about the cardinal. When Wolsey returned to see Henry the following morning, he found the king about to leave for a jaunt with Anne. Henry explained he had no time to chat and rode off. Wolsey never saw him again.

Two days later Wolsey was ordered to surrender the great seal, the symbol of his office as lord chancellor of England. At the same time Henry seized Wolsey's great mansions at Hampton Court and elsewhere and banished the cardinal to a small palace.

But this was not all. On October 9, Wolsey was accused of violating the Statute of Praemunire. This act, which had been passed in 1353, said that anyone who appealed abroad a case that should be tried in the king's courts was guilty of treason. Now Wolsey was accused of treason for exercising his functions as papal legate in England, even though he had done everything with the king's approval.

At the time of his downfall, Wolsey was fifty-eight years old; he was to live another year hoping in vain to be restored to the king's favor. Henry encouraged this dream by sending the cardinal gifts and friendly messages and by pardoning him for the praemunire charge. After a while Wolsey's enemies at court began to fear that Henry longed for his competent minister and might return him to power. "To reinstate him in the king's favor would not be difficult," wrote the new Imperial ambassador, Eustache Chapuys, "if it were not for [Anne Boleyn]." She was seconded by the nobles who never forgave Wolsey for usurping their place at the king's side. The duke of Norfolk growled that rather than let Wolsey return to power, he would "eat him up alive."

The cardinal's enemies decided to move him so far from court that the king would forget him. Accordingly it was suggested to Henry that since Wolsey had been archbishop of York for some fifteen years without ever setting foot in his diocese, it would be both fitting and holy to send him north to watch over his flock. Northern England was always a rebellious area; perhaps Wolsey could enforce the king's rule there. In any case, he would be some two hundred miles distant, and even if his presence did little for York, his absence would do a lot for London.

Henry agreed to send Wolsey north, and so in his last days the cardinal became what he had never been before, a priest. In his new mood of penitence, Wolsey took to wearing a hair shirt beneath his robes. Poverty was no problem because the king had seized everything he owned; he had even dissolved the school Wolsey built at Ipswich.

At York, Wolsey was a good cleric, saying mass, settling quarrels, living modestly. The people came to respect him, to the surprise of practically everyone. But his success hastened his ending. His enemies feared more than ever that he might return to power, particularly since the king had taken to reminding his councillors that not one of them was as good as Wolsey. Rumors haunted the court that the cardinal intended to resume power, that he intended to flee, that he was secretly plotting with Rome.

Henry listened to the rumors and the accusations, especially when they came from the sweet lips of Anne Boleyn. On November 4, 1530, the earl of Northumberland came to Wolsey's palace at York. The earl was Henry Percy, the young man Wolsey had once ordered to forget Anne Boleyn. Trembling with the weight of his mission, the earl put his hand on the old man's arm and said softly, "My lord, I arrest you of high treason." The charge was that Wolsey had "intrigued" with Francis, Charles, and Clement to restore himself to power.

Under guard the man who had ruled England for fourteen years set out for London to be tried and executed. Thousands of the people whose hearts he had unexpectedly won stood at his gate cursing his enemies and shouting, "God save your Grace!"

God did save his Grace, at least from the axeman. While Wolsey was still one hundred miles from London, he became seriously ill. He and his guards rode to the Abbey of St. Mary of the Meadows, north of the city of Leicester. When Wolsey reached the gate he said to the abbot, "I am come hither to leave my bones among you."

By the morning of November 28, Wolsey lay dying. He asked one of his servants what time it was. The servant said it was after eight. "Nay, nay, it cannot be eight of the clock," murmured Wolsey, "for by eight of the clock you will lose your master."

At dawn the following morning Wolsey made his final confession. Afterward he spoke his most memorable lines. "If I had served God as diligently as I have done the king," he said, "He would not have given me over in my gray hairs."

As the clock struck eight that morning, Thomas Cardinal Wolsey died. Except in the north of England, few wept. At the court, Anne Boleyn and her friends celebrated with a play called *Of the Cardinal's Going to Hell*. Most of the common people were just as rude. It is believed that it was the fall and death of Cardinal Wolsey that set them to chanting:

> *Humpty Dumpty sat on a wall,*
> *Humpty Dumpty had a great fall;*
> *All the king's horses,*
> *And all the king's men,*
> *Couldn't put Humpty Dumpty together again.*

Henry might rejoice at Wolsey's death, but it brought him no nearer an annulment. Not that he wasn't trying. In the summer of 1529, Fox and Gardiner, the two men who had gone to Orvieto to plead with Clement, met Thomas Cranmer, a mild-mannered Cambridge don who had an interesting idea. He suggested that the universities in England and on the continent be polled to see whether the scholars and theologians thought Henry could legally marry his brother's widow. The weight of their opinion, which would surely be in Henry's favor, might sway the papacy.

By now Henry was getting desperate enough to try anything. "Who is this Doctor Cranmer?" he cried. "This man . . . has got the right sow by the ear!" Cranmer was made chaplain to Anne Boleyn, and English agents were sent to the universities to seek and purchase opinions in Henry's behalf. The man who won the title "Defender of the Faith" for his attack on Martin Luther even had the archheretic himself queried, but the answer brought no comfort. Luther felt Henry had been obliged to marry Catherine, as set forth in Deuteronomy.

In the summer the king also decided to summon Parliament. It was to sit on and off for seven years and come to be called the Reformation Parliament, since its primary purpose, as far as Henry was concerned, was to pass more and more anticlerical measures until Clement surrendered and granted the annulment.

The first session met on November 3, 1529. A week earlier, Henry had chosen Sir Thomas More to succeed Wolsey as lord chancellor. More was a lawyer not a cleric, so church and state would not reside in the same official until they came to rest in Henry himself. More was also a noted writer, humanist philosopher, and diplomat; he had one of the keenest minds of his age. Unlike Wolsey, he was neither greedy nor corrupt. Because of his intellectual luster he would add much to Henry's court, and because of his honesty he would take nothing away.

Unfortunately, if the king had a conscience, so had More. More had been publicly silent on the king's great matter, but everyone, including Henry, knew that More disapproved of the annulment. Henry therefore promised his new chancellor that the annulment would be pressed by men who were sympathetic to it and that he would "never with that matter molest his conscience." He graciously told More that he "should look first unto God, and after God unto him." Eventually, Henry would reverse the order.

One of the reasons Henry had summoned Parliament was to raise money, which he perpetually needed, and to free him from repaying the huge sums Wolsey had borrowed for him from his subjects. However, he was well aware there was substantial anticlerical feeling in England and he meant to use it to pressure the church until it bent to his will.

The members of Parliament were generally upper and middle-class landowners and merchants, who had the greatest grievances against the church. They were not heretics, for most of them were too beef-witted to understand the theological disputes of the age. They were anticlerical in challenging the political and financial power of the church, which they coveted for themselves. They also

92

resented flagrant clerical abuses, such as undisguised corruption and exorbitant fees, as well as the very fact that the church was directed by a foreign power that was more political than spiritual.

Parliament cooperated with the king and his council, but not without small bursts of independence. The members forgave the king his debts but did not grant him new taxes. However, they did move toward clerical reform by limiting church fees for certain services and prohibiting certain abuses. The bishops in the house of Lords, led by John Fisher, protested bitterly. They wanted reform but they felt it should come from within the church. They feared that if it was applied by secular force, it would escalate from correcting petty abuses to challenging basic theology and the church would be destroyed.

But the bills passed, and the state established its power to legislate for the church. In England, in Henry's time, the Reformation would come not as a repudiation of church dogma, as it was on the continent, but as an affirmation that the church was subservient to the state. It would be the victory of the concept of a national church over the medieval concept of a universal church.

During the early months of 1530, Cranmer's plan for polling the universities was being busily carried out. In many places Henry's agents could get what they wanted only with threats, pleas, or bribes; at Oxford, two of them were stoned. As soon as the Imperialists learned of the project, they began issuing their own threats and bribes. Most of the opinions, for or against the annulment, were paid for by one side or the other, and it was profitable to be a scholar that spring.

In this particular battle for men's hearts and minds, the pope put himself directly behind Charles. In March he issued a bull which threatened Henry with excommunication if he married again. Two weeks later he issued another bull forbidding church scholars to speak or write against the validity of Henry's marriage.

In return Henry became more defiant. He had his agents in Rome tell the pope that neither the king nor any other Englishman could be forced to submit to a foreign power. He demanded that the case be settled by the English clergy; since he couldn't control the Roman courts, he wanted the case settled by courts he could control. But the pope rejected Henry's claim that Rome had no jurisdiction in the case. Popes had always been called upon to settle the matrimonial problems of kings, including kings of England.

Both sides hardened their positions. By the end of the year, Henry was asserting "we know no superior on earth." He was also leaning on a new adviser named Thomas Cromwell. Cromwell was the lawyer who had dissolved certain monasteries for Cardinal Wolsey. Complaints of Cromwell's cruel and corrupt behavior came all the way back to the king and marked him forever as a very useful man.

When Wolsey was first banished, Cromwell was one of those who went with him. One day Wolsey's faithful aide, George Cavendish, saw Cromwell standing by a window with a prayer book in hand, weeping.

"Why, Master Cromwell," said Cavendish, "is my lord in any danger for whom ye lament thus?"

"Nay," said Cromwell candidly, "it is my own unhappy case, that I am like to lose all I have worked for all the days of my life."

But Cromwell made it clear he did not propose to sink with Wolsey. "I intend, God willing, to ride to London, and so to court," he told Cavendish, "where I will make or mar e'er I come again."

Cromwell clambered up the slippery rungs of royal favor rapidly. Sometime in the autumn of 1530 he is supposed to have advised the king to marry Anne Boleyn and renounce the pope. This was not new; it had been suggested to Henry many times, mostly by Anne herself. But Cromwell had something more to say. He told the king to declare himself head of the church in England, with the consent of Parliament. England, said Cromwell, was a monster with two heads, king and pope. If the king assumed religious as well as secular power, the clergy would become responsible to him and England would have just one head.

Henry liked the idea. He made Cromwell a member of his council and intensified his campaign against the church. First, he had fifteen clerics cited on the charge of praemunire, which had been used against Wolsey. Praemunire was a valuable weapon because the statute was so vaguely worded it could be applied almost at will. Chapuys, the Imperial ambassador, wrote, "Its interpretation lies solely in the king's head, who amplifies it and declares it at his pleasure, making it apply to any case he pleases."

The fifteen churchmen, who included Bishop John Fisher and others sympathetic to Catherine, were charged with complicity in Wolsey's guilt. Then Henry changed his mind. The charge against the fifteen was withdrawn and a praemunire charge was prepared against the whole clergy of England for having ecclesiastical courts in the country.

Both Parliament and Convocation, a meeting of the English

clergy, convened in January, 1531. The clergy knew they were being blackmailed and they submitted. They paid Henry a huge sum of money, after which he pardoned them, and the ecclesiastical courts went on as before. But the king was not through; for once he wanted more than just money. As the next step the churchmen were told to acknowledge Henry as "Protector and Supreme Head of the church in England."

As far as the clergy were concerned, the supreme head of the church, not only in England but everywhere, was the pope. As a compromise William Warham, the archbishop of Canterbury, suggested that Henry be called, "The singular Protector, the only Supreme Lord, and as far as was permitted by the law of Christ, even the Supreme Head." None of the clergy meeting in Convocation responded to this. "He that is silent seems to consent," said Warham. "Then are we all silent," cried a voice.

No one was quite sure what the new title meant. Chapuys said the king planned to be pope in England, but Henry scoffed at such an interpretation. He said he claimed no power over spiritual things, but only in the temporal dealings of spiritual persons. In February he was still assuring a papal representative that he would respect papal authority as long as the pope "had for him the regard he was entitled to." For the moment, the new title was just another club to beat Clement into submission. There would be no break with the church if Henry could only have his way.

While Parliament was in session that spring, someone tried to poison Bishop John Fisher, who was leading the fight against Henry both in the house of Lords and in Convocation. One night in March a dozen people who ate dinner at Fisher's home fell ill.

Several died and the bishop was seriously ill for a month.

Under torture Fisher's cook confessed that he had seasoned the soup with a pinch of poison, but he would not say who had asked or paid him to do it. Henry feared poison, for it was too democratic a killer. Only the king could use the axe against his enemies, but any of his enemies could use poison against the king. A law was passed condemning poisoners to be burned alive, and the cook was its first victim. If anyone knew who had plotted against Fisher, however, he did not speak out. No one suspected Henry, but both at court and in the market place suspicion fell on Anne Boleyn.

People didn't suspect Henry because murder was not usually his way. He was still trying to bludgeon an annulment from Rome in the loudest possible manner and trying to get his own countrymen to support him. He had no more success at home than he had abroad.

At the end of March, Henry's treasurer appeared before Lords to plead with them to support the annulment. He was greeted with such opposition and hostility that he tried his luck in Commons. There he met a wall of silence. The next day Henry prorogued, or adjourned, Parliament.

After Parliament declined to act, Henry turned to the aged archbishop of Canterbury, the nation's highest churchman, and asked him to try the case. But Warham refused, for the pope had specifically forbidden him to do so.

Henry was getting nowhere. Anne Boleyn constantly prodded him to "declare the pope a heretic" and marry her, but the king was reluctant to break with Rome. As long as he could fight the case he would, hoping eventually to win papal consent. Of course, during this prolonged period, England had no certain heir, since it was critical to Henry's argument to proclaim Mary illegitimate.

Henry had reason to hope for ultimate victory, however, for, although the pope had recalled the case to Rome in 1529, little had been done about it since. Clement wanted to keep Charles happy, so he refused to grant an annulment, but he didn't really want to make an enemy of Henry, so he didn't decide the case in Catherine's favor. He was afraid the willful monarch would cause a schism in the church and perhaps follow the German princes into Lutheranism, so he steered a cautious course, hoping to offend no one any more than necessary.

Clement did not realize that his inaction and vacillation weakened the church in England. Nothing positive that he could have done was as infuriating to the English as his doing nothing at all. Most of the people supported Catherine; when the pope equivocated, he diminished not their faith in Christ but their respect for the papacy.

While Henry was at work pressuring the pope, he was also pressuring and threatening Catherine to make her more compliant. On May 31, he sent a large delegation of nobles to speak to her. Afterward the duke of Suffolk told the king, "The queen is ready to obey you in everything, except for the obedience she owes two higher powers."

"The emperor and the pope?" asked Henry.

"No, sire," replied Suffolk, "God and her conscience."

Henry found this intolerable since the only conscience that counted was his. A few weeks later, the entire court, including

Henry, Catherine, and Anne, moved to Windsor Castle. On the morning of July 11, without a word of farewell, Henry left Catherine and rode off with Anne Boleyn. He never returned, and Catherine never saw him again. Not long after, Henry ordered Catherine to choose a house to retire to. He later ordered her to part from her daughter Mary, then sixteen, and they never saw each other again.

The news that Henry had actually deserted Catherine aroused the country. People praised the queen and muttered unprintable epithets about Anne Boleyn. Concerned, Henry ordered every priest in the kingdom to speak out for him. Few responded and one who did was pulled from his pulpit by an outraged congregation.

When Parliament met again in January, 1532, the members were cold to proposals offered by the king that his case be heard in an English ecclesiastical or temporal court. One man in Commons spoke openly against the annulment. After five years of challenging church and country for what was becoming little more than the pursuit of his ego, the king stood almost alone.

But if the king had few friends, neither did the church, and this Henry would now exploit. Cromwell initiated the newest assault by preparing what was called the "Supplication of the Commons against the Ordinaries." In this document, which originated with Cromwell, not Parliament, Commons protested the fact that the clergy made laws independent of the laws of the realm. Specific clerical abuses were cited and action was begged of the king, "in whom and by whom the only and sole redress, reformation, and remedy herein absolutely rests and remains."

At the same time Henry was driving a wedge between Commons and the clergy, he was trying to get Lords to pass a bill which would greatly reduce annates, the fees bishops paid to Rome when they were consecrated. The bill passed, but it was not to go into effect until Henry approved it. Since annates were a principal source of papal revenue, the threat of enforcing the bill was still another weapon for Henry to use against Rome.

Meanwhile the Supplication was passed along to Convocation, the meeting of the clergy. The churchmen admitted there were abuses, but said they had been making church laws independent of England for hundreds of years, it was their duty to decide on matters of faith and morals, and they were doing nothing contrary to the laws of England.

This did not satisfy Henry. He informed Parliament that he had discovered the clergy belonged only half to him, "for the prelates at their consecration make an oath to the pope clean contrary to the oath they make to us, so that they seem his subjects and not ours." What was astonishing about Henry's discovery was not that the clergy took an oath to the pope, but that Henry should have pretended to have just discovered it after reigning for twenty-three years. He suggested Parliament act to correct what he implied was treason on the part of the whole clergy. But before the members did, they were prorogued.

There was really no need for Parliament to do anything. Convocation was so cowed by this threat of a mass treason charge that the clergy surrendered. On May 15 the clerics agreed that church laws, old and new, would not be valid without the king's consent. The church was no longer universal or independent in England; it was a tool of the king's.

The day after the historic "Submission of the Clergy,"

Thomas More resigned as lord chancellor. He believed that the church needed reform, but if it was failing in the hands of an Italian prince, it would do no better in the hands of the English king. A few days later More said to Cromwell, "If you will follow my poor advice, you shall in your counsel-giving unto his Grace, ever tell him what he ought do so, and never what he is able to do. . . . For if a lion knew his own strength, hard were it for any man to rule him."

More's advice came too late, for the lion already knew his strength. He decided it was time to be rid of William Warham. A more pliable archbishop of Canterbury would be more helpful in the king's great matter. Henry reached for his favorite weapon; the eighty-two-year-old cleric was cited for praemunire. Warham dictated his defense, in which he intended to say, "It were, indeed, as good to have no spirituality as to have it at the prince's pleasure." But the old man died a natural death before he could be brought to trial.

Henry's path was finally swept clear. A sympathetic archbishop would grant the annulment and the pope could fret about it afterward. Henry knew just the man for the job. He was Thomas Cranmer, formerly chaplain to Anne Boleyn and presently ambassador to the emperor, the Cambridge don who had suggested polling the universities on Henry's behalf.

Henry now moved to conciliate the pope, who had to approve the appointment of the new archbishop. He pointedly reminded Clement that he was withholding his consent from the act that would reduce his rich income from annates.

The king's next step was to refurbish his alliance with Francis, for if the worst happened, Charles might decide to make war in defense of his aunt's honor. Henry wanted to meet Francis to work out all the details of their new friendship and to exhibit Anne as his future queen; he even ordered Catherine to surrender her jewels to her successor.

The meeting was held in Boulogne in October, 1532. Henry did not want Francis to bring his Spanish queen, who was Catherine's niece, and Francis' sister refused to have anything to do with Anne Boleyn, so Henry was forced to leave Anne in Calais and go to Boulogne without her. There he dropped money and jewels into the right purses and cancelled some of the debts France owed England. In return Francis promised to send two French cardinals to reason with Clement and to help make sure the new archbishop was approved.

At the same time Cranmer was summoned home from the continent, where he had just been married, a somewhat awkward situation for a future archbishop of Canterbury. Catherine and Chapuys, the Imperial ambassador, begged the pope to bar the nomination, for they knew Cranmer would dissolve Henry's marriage. Nonetheless, in March, 1533, the appointment was approved.

No one knows exactly why, any more than anyone knows exactly why any or all of the major characters acted as they did during the tedious, tangled crisis of the annulment. Perhaps Clement believed Cranmer would move only after the case had been heard elsewhere. Perhaps he did not believe Cranmer would defy him. Perhaps he knew that Cranmer would indeed defy him and was satisfied to have the whole thing done with, by someone else, so Charles could not hold him responsible. Perhaps he thought the case would continue to drag on and on until death provided a solution. Or perhaps he hoped that if he confirmed Cranmer, Henry would not confirm the bill reducing annates.

In any case, the pope could not know what lay in the future. He also did not know how urgent Henry's great matter had suddenly become for, by the beginning of 1533, Anne Boleyn was pregnant.

# 9 ⮀ Lord, King, and Husband

FOR SIX YEARS or more, Anne Boleyn lived in Henry's palaces and traveled with him on his journeys, so everyone supposed she was his mistress. But she was not. She had decided that the price of surrender would be the crown, and with a determination as strong as Henry's or Catherine's she did not waver.

Henry called his love "my great folly" and if the crown was her price, he would pay it. All of England could loathe him, all of Europe could laugh at him, his enemies could threaten him with war and the pope could threaten him with excommunication, but he would make Anne Boleyn his wife. But in defying all earthly and spiritual powers to gain what he wished, Henry may not have been driven as much by his love of Anne Boleyn as he was by his love of himself. What he really wanted was not a particular woman but his own way.

No one knows exactly when Anne finally surrendered to Henry, or why. The death of Warham and the selection of Cranmer may have been sufficient warranty for her future. Or she may have feared the king was losing interest in the chase and the only way to capture him was with the promise of a son.

Whatever her reasons, Anne Boleyn was Henry's mistress by the end of 1532, and in January, 1533, she told him she was pregnant. The king knew he had to move at once. His heir— his son—had to be legitimate. Nothing must mar the birth of the successor to the throne.

On or about January 25, 1533, Henry and Anne were married in such secrecy that no one is certain who performed the ceremony or where it was held. Secrecy was vital because the king was still married to his first wife, and he needed the help of pope, Parliament, and Canterbury to free himself.

By March, Rome had confirmed Cranmer's appointment. Parliament was already in session, and under massive pressure from the king, both houses passed the Act in Restraint of Appeals. Henceforth all spiritual causes, including marriage and annulment, would be judged in England, not Rome. Final judgment rested with Canterbury or Convocation; no one could appeal to the pope. Now Henry had the judge he wanted, and Catherine was forbidden to appeal to Rome. There was just one more item to attend to.

The Act in Restraint of Appeals would have permitted Catherine to appeal to Convocation. Therefore, at the same time the act was being pushed through Parliament, Convocation passed a motion that no pope could permit the marriage of a man with his brother's widow. Henry had arranged matters so there was no longer any justice in England for Catherine, and no way she could get it elsewhere.

All that remained was for Cranmer to see to the last details.

He had to work rapidly because Anne's secret was a secret no longer. One day late in February, in a room full of courtiers, she told the poet Thomas Wyatt that she had a furious longing to eat apples, and the king had told her this was a sign that she was pregnant. Then she ran from the room laughing hysterically.

With the scene court gossip, Henry formally announced the marriage to his council. On April 9 he sent the duke of Norfolk to tell Catherine she was no longer queen. On April 11 Cranmer wrote Henry for permission to try the king's case, and Henry graciously consented.

On May 8 Cranmer called his court to order. On May 23 he declared Henry's marriage to Catherine void because her previous marriage had been consummated. On May 28 Cranmer announced that he had investigated Henry's marriage to Anne Boleyn and found it valid. On June 1 Anne Boleyn was crowned queen of England.

But all the costly and elaborate pageants and celebrations could not conceal the hostility of the people. After the procession to Westminster, Henry said to Anne, "How like you the look of the city, sweetheart?" And Anne, whose eyes were as sharp as her tongue, replied, "Sir, the city itself was well enough, but I saw so many caps on heads and heard but few tongues. . . ." The people would not bare their heads for their new queen, and it was just as well that she could not hear what they were calling her.

Now that Catherine had lost her long battle to save her honor and her daughter's inheritance, she would do nothing but submit to the will of God. Chapuys, Charles's ambassador in England and Catherine's devoted friend, begged the emperor to declare war. He said that if Charles acted at once, the whole kingdom would rise up to join him.

But Catherine overruled Chapuys. She said she would rather die than be cause for war. Since Charles had many other problems in his vast empire, he chose to listen to his aunt rather than his ambassador. He would not even agree to cut off trade with England, since this would hurt the Netherlands. "The emperor could ruin us all if he liked," said the wily Cromwell, "but what good would that do the emperor?"

But prodded by Anne, Henry was uneasy about Catherine. He sent a deputation of nobles to ask her to accept the title of "princess dowager," all that was due her as Arthur's widow. If she submitted, she would be well cared for. If she did not, she would be inciting the people to rebellion and she and her daughter might suffer for it.

Catherine took the document the deputation had brought. With a pen she crossed out the words "princess dowager" and substituted the word "queen." She said she was the king's wife and not his harlot, and that she was not stirring treason in his realm. If she were, she would be content to accept the punishment. "For since I have brought England little good," she told the nobles, "I should be the loather to bring it any harm."

When Thomas Cromwell heard of Catherine's spirited reply, he said, "Nature wronged the queen in not making her a man. But for her sex, she would have surpassed all the heroes of history."

Henry, however, was not impressed, for he simply could not bear to be bested in an argument. "God, who knows my righteous heart, always prospers my affairs," he once said. For a man so certain of his alliance with God, Henry needed a great deal of reassurance. Catherine would not agree to the wisdom of calling her a concubine, so he exiled her to a dismal castle to reconsider. Then he turned to the pope.

Having challenged and insulted Clement for years, having all but abolished papal power in England, having defied Rome by marrying Anne Boleyn, Henry now tried to win approval for what he had done. To strengthen his arguments, he put into effect the Act in Restraint of Annates, which cut off most of the papal income from England.

But Henry had gone too far, even for Clement. On July 11 Clement condemned Henry's second marriage and threatened to excommunicate him if he did not go back to Catherine by September.

Henry had no intention of going back to Catherine ever, and certainly not in September, when his son was due. For it would be a son; he had no doubt of that. He had consulted doctors, astrologers, soothsayers, and mystics of every sort, and they all had assured him, for a fee, that he would have a son. Henry even had a proclamation prepared announcing the birth of the prince.

The child was born on the afternoon of September 7, 1533. It was a girl.

The infant was called Elizabeth, after Henry's mother. England's greatest queen was, at birth, its most unwanted child. But Henry tried to put the best possible face on the disaster. He named Elizabeth princess of Wales, which had been the title of his daughter Mary, now seventeen. Mary was ordered to call the infant "princess"; she replied that she would call her "sister" and nothing else. "I know of no other princess but myself," said the daughter of Catherine of Aragon. Thus, all that Henry had accomplished was to put the succession to the throne in even greater jeopardy by producing two daughters representing two different factions, each considering the other illegitimate.

If Henry was disappointed by the birth of a daughter, Anne Boleyn suffered doubly. All she ever had to offer the king was herself, and once he had her he turned to other women. Within months of his second marriage, Henry had a new mistress and when Anne berated him Henry sharply told her to shut her eyes and endure it as her betters had done. Anne now knew she could hold onto the king only if she bore him a son. When Elizabeth was born, Anne Boleyn may finally have understood how Catherine of Aragon had felt.

When September came and Henry did not return to Catherine, the pope did not excommunicate him. He was still opposed to losing Henry and England to the church. Again Henry demanded that Clement finally decide the case in his favor, but this the pope would not do. In March, 1534, Rome declared that Catherine was Henry's legal wife.

The verdict came seven years too late. It brought some comfort to Catherine, but it had no meaning in England. For by the time Clement finally acted, Henry had gotten weary of submitting to someone who would not agree with him. If the pope would not give him what he wanted, he would take Cromwell's advice and make himself pope.

But first the people had to be prepared and so did Parliament. The presses churned out broadsides attacking the church and hailing the new marriage. Every preacher in England was ordered to add his voice to the chorus. When Parliament assembled in January, 1534, friends of Catherine and the church were absent, for they had been forbidden to attend. John Fisher came anyway, but few had his courage.

Henry needed Parliament in 1534 to complete his break with Rome. To make the members pliable, Thomas Cromwell used the weapon of simple terror. His instrument was an epileptic mystic named Elizabeth Barton.

Elizabeth Barton was a nun who had trances and made prophecies. She became known as the Holy Maid of Kent and, in an age that believed in spirits, she developed a considerable following. People made pilgrimages to her convent in Canterbury to seek her guidance and hear her revelations.

Unfortunately for the Holy Maid, her prophecies on the matter of the annulment were unacceptable, since she had predicted that if Henry married Anne, he would die. Such talk was treason, and Cromwell decided to make the most of it.

In July, 1533, the Holy Maid was questioned by Cranmer. Her reputation and her words had sped far beyond the convent, and fear seized even the most prominent men and women in the kingdom, who dreaded being found guilty of some remote association with her. To multiply the panic, Cromwell did not publish a list of suspects, but let it be known there were many of them.

When Parliament met in January, 1534, the government brought in a bill of attainder against the Holy Maid. Attainder dispensed with the right to trial and provided for the execution of a subject by consent of Parliament and king.

Among those named in the bill of attainder with the Holy Maid, to be executed without trial, were Thomas More and Bishop John Fisher. When More demanded the right to defend himself, his name and Fisher's were removed from the list, but if the two greatest men in England could be condemned by association, no one could be sure of his safety. When the Holy Maid was finally put to death for treason, only five others died with her. It was not necessary to execute anyone else at that time, for by then a thoroughly intimidated Parliament had given Henry and Cromwell exactly what they wanted.

London and Rome were severed by a series of parliamentary acts. The Act in Restraint of Annates of 1532 was bolstered by a new act which halted the payment of all annates to Rome and decreed that in the future all bishops and archbishops would be appointed by the king, without confirmation by Rome. Another act provided that Canterbury, not Rome, would hereafter issue dispensations and other church documents. It also affirmed the king's right to visit and reform religious houses in the realm.

A third act went further than the Act in Restraint of Appeals. It said that one could appeal from Canterbury's court only to the king's Court of Chancery. Thus, not only was Roman control of church justice ended, but clerical control also. A fourth act said it was no longer heresy to deny the primacy of the pope.

The Act of Succession declared the king's first marriage null, provided that the throne should pass to the children of Henry and Anne, and made it high treason to question the king's second marriage or the succession by "writing, print, deed, or act." Nor was silence acceptable. Every subject was required to take an oath accepting the Act of Succession.

The work of dividing the church in England from Rome was completed when Parliament met again in November and passed the Act of the Supreme Head. It declared that "the king's Majesty justly and rightfully is and ought to be the Supreme Head of the Church of England." Henry no longer had need of a pope; he had made himself pope. The church in England was no longer part of the universal Roman Catholic Church; it had become a new, independent entity, the Church of England. At the same time, Parliament put teeth in the Act of Succession by spelling out the terms of the oath everyone had to take and the penalties for failing to do so.

Although there was some opposition in Parliament, these acts passed without much difficulty. The members were more than a little cowed by the probability that any serious objections would open them to charges of treason; the fate of the Holy Maid of Kent stayed fresh in their minds. "Fear compelled us to bear with the times," said one contemporary.

But there were other reasons. Each act taken separately seemed sensible and useful. Many of the members were incapable of viewing the cumulative effects of the legislation and realizing they were making a revolution. For the practices of the church were, for the moment, untouched. In fact, one of the acts asserted that "the king and all his natural subjects . . . be as devout, catholic, and humble children of God and Holy Church, as any people be within any realm christened." As long as their religion was undisturbed, it didn't matter who received the payments or appointed the bishops. Most Englishmen would prefer to see the money and power kept in the kingdom rather than given to a foreigner.

As for the Act of Succession, many people felt it was the king's business to choose his heirs, although the preamble was troubling. It repudiated the pope's decision on the king's first marriage, so to swear to the preamble was to deny the authority of the pope. Not to swear to it, however, was treason.

There followed a swift, merciless reign of terror, while Henry and his henchmen rooted out those who would not swear to the succession. The first victims were the friars and monks. Many took the oath, but those who resisted were imprisoned and tortured. Some suffered the traitor's death of being drawn and quartered while still alive.

At the same time he was hanging those who denied his papacy, Henry was burning those who went too far and preached Protestant heresies. No view was permitted except the king's, and every man who was not entirely for him became his enemy.

Among those who could not accept Henry's view of his own divinity were John Fisher and Thomas More. Fisher, now seventy-four, had been a burr in Henry's side for years. The long, lean churchman had a conscience a lot firmer than Henry's, and much less self-serving. He believed in God, the universal church, and the pope, and he said bluntly that the king could not possibly be supreme head on earth of the church in England. In April, 1534, when he refused to take the oath of succession, he was thrown into the Tower of London, a combination fortress, palace, and prison.

In September of that year, Pope Clement died. The new pope, Paul III, made the imprisoned bishop a cardinal. Henry said viciously that he would send Fisher's head to Rome for his cardinal's hat, and he all but kept his word. On June 22, 1535, Fisher went to the block clutching a Bible in his withered hands. His severed head was not sent to Rome, but it was impaled on a pike atop London Bridge.

Not even England's most illustrious figure could escape Henry's wrath. Years earlier, Henry had asked Thomas More to serve as lord chancellor, promising not to "molest his conscience." When More realized he could not serve both his king and his conscience, he resigned. He opposed the annulment but, unlike the courageous Fisher, he did not speak against it publicly. Yet when the Act of Succession passed, Henry demanded that More swear to it.

Like Fisher, More believed there had to be a higher morality than the king's, especially this one. More was willing to swear to the Act of Succession but not to the preamble, which repudiated the pope. Archbishop Cranmer charitably suggested that both More and Fisher be permitted to swear to the succession only, omitting the preamble. But Henry would not be only partially right.

More was tried on July 1, 1535, and found guilty on perjured evidence. He was beheaded on the morning of July 6, after saying that he died the king's good servant, but God's first.

Sixteenth-century Europe was too steeped in blood and horror to be aroused by ordinary butchery, but the deaths of Fisher and More shocked the continent. Erasmus now wrote, "In England, death has either snatched everyone away or fear has shrunk them up." Emperor Charles said, "I would rather have lost the best city in my dominions than such a counsellor as More."

But Henry, cushioned in the womb of his ego, was impervious to criticism. Driven by fear, guilt, vanity, and Anne Boleyn's taunts, he tried to eliminate anyone who might oppose him, and that included Catherine. "The lady Catherine is a proud, stubborn woman of very high courage," he told his council one day. "She could quite easily take the field, muster a great array, and wage against me a war as fierce as any her mother Isabella ever waged in Spain."

To prevent this, Henry threatened Catherine with death unless she swore to the Act of Succession. She calmly refused, saying, "I ask only that I be allowed to die in the sight of the people." But that was the last thing Henry would permit, for the execution of the beloved queen would be certain to spark a rebellion. He didn't even dare to put her in the Tower, so he kept her prisoner in a distant castle.

His daughter Mary also refused to take the oath that proclaimed her illegitimate, although she was later forced to. Henry was so fearful of what mother and daughter might accomplish if they were together that he refused to let them see each other, even when both were seriously ill. Mary was continually harassed and threatened by Anne Boleyn, who said pointedly, "If I have a son, as I hope shortly, I know what will become of her." When Mary became ill early in 1535, there was some suspicion that Anne had tried to have her poisoned.

Mary would live to see what became of Anne Boleyn, but Catherine would not. She died on the afternoon of January 7, 1536. Although there were the inevitable rumors of poison, she appears to have had cancer.

The morning of her death, Catherine dictated her last letter to Henry. She saluted him as "My most dear lord, king, and husband." She said she forgave him for all he had done to her and begged him to be a good father to their daughter Mary. Her last words to him were, "I make this vow, that mine eyes desire you above all things." And then she signed the letter, "Catherine, queen of England."

# 10 ~ False Traitors and Rebels

LIKE MOST tyrants Henry had a sentimental side. He wept when he read Catherine's last letter, then he and Anne dressed gaily in yellow and celebrated her death with a ball. At the festivities Henry walked about with the child Elizabeth in his arms saying, "God be praised, the old harridan is dead. Now there is no fear of war."

Anne was just as joyful. "Now I am at last a queen!" she exulted. But she did not realize that Henry was happy because Catherine's death had freed him from both women. The king had quickly grown tired of Anne. Like Catherine she had failed to produce a son. The daughter Elizabeth had been followed by miscarriages.

"I am her death, as she is mine," said Anne of Catherine, when she finally understood Henry's feelings. On the day that Catherine was buried, Anne gave birth to a stillborn son. Her fate was sealed. Henry was still being denied sons; the fault must be Anne's, just as it had been Catherine's. Henry would never believe the problem might be his. He was to have six wives and many mistresses, yet he fathered only four children. But this could not be the king's fault. Once when Chapuys asked him how he could be so sure of having sons if he married Anne, he shouted angrily, "Am I not a man like other men?"

If Anne could not produce sons, all it meant was that Henry needed a new wife, and he had someone in mind. He had chosen her as early as 1534, a year after his second marriage. Her name was Jane Seymour, and she was a quiet woman of the court who had been a lady-in-waiting to Henry's first two queens. Possibly Jane's greatest attraction was that she was plain, kind, and good, which contrasted sharply with the mercurial, shrewish Anne Boleyn.

Anne was safe as long as Catherine lived, for if the king cast her aside, it would imply that the pope was right, and if the pope was right, Henry would be expected to take Catherine back. As soon as Catherine was safely dead, Henry ordered Cromwell to free him of Anne Boleyn as well. Since another annulment would only create more arguments and discord, there was only one way; Anne had to die.

Cromwell sifted through the layers of court dirt and before long he accused Anne of adultery with six men and incest with her brother George. This was treason for all concerned, since it could produce a questionable heir to the throne.

Charges against two of the men were dropped, but the other four were tried on May 12, 1536. Anne and her brother were tried three days later by a court headed by their uncle, the duke of Norfolk.

Anne and all but one of the men declared their innocence, and the one who confessed had been tortured. All were found guilty, and the five men were executed on May 17. Anne was beheaded two days later by an axeman brought especially from the continent. This was Henry's last kindness for the woman for whom he had jeopardized his throne and his soul.

Anne Boleyn was guilty of many things, but adultery was probably not one of them. She was murdered to make way for the next queen. Her brother was murdered not because he had committed incest but to prevent him from avenging her death.

Henry's oft-cited conscience did not flinch at what he knew was judicial murder. He was glad to be rid of Anne. He said she had bewitched him. One night Henry told his illegitimate son, the duke of Richmond, with the tears of self-pity that came so easily to his eyes, that the youth and his sister Mary were lucky to have escaped Anne, who had tried to poison them both. Henry did not feel guilt for what he had done to Anne Boleyn, any more than he felt guilt for what he had done to others on her behalf.

Two days before Anne's execution, the amenable archbishop of Canterbury, Thomas Cranmer, pronounced Henry's marriage to Anne invalid, because Anne's sister had been Henry's mistress. Cranmer had of course known this when he declared the marriage valid only three years earlier. Besides, if Anne had never been married to Henry, she could not be guilty of adultery, but this was too subtle a point for Tudor justice.

On the day of Anne's death, Cranmer granted Henry a dispensation to wed Jane Seymour, which was necessary because they were distantly related. They were married on May 30.

By the Act of Succession of 1534, which had cost England some of its finest heads, the children of Anne Boleyn were to succeed to the throne. Obviously this error had to be rectified, so a new Parliament was summoned in the summer of 1536. A new Act of Succession made Elizabeth as illegitimate as Mary and destined the crown for the children of Jane Seymour. Should there be none, Henry could name as heir anyone he chose. Perhaps he had in mind his illegitimate son, the duke of Richmond, but the seventeen-year-old youth died of tuberculosis that summer. Thus, for all of his frantic attempts to secure his dynasty, Henry had, at the age of forty-five, no sons and only two daughters, both of whom he had declared illegitimate.

If there was still considerable doubt about who would rule England when Henry died, there was no question about who would rule its church while he lived. At the end of 1534, Parliament had passed a law saying that annates, those burdensome payments forbidden to Rome, would now be collected by the crown, along with an annual tax of one-tenth the income of all benefices. To determine how much money the church should pay him, however, Henry first had to determine how much it had.

As supreme head, Henry had appointed Cromwell vicar-general to oversee his church. Unlike Wolsey, Cromwell was not a cardinal; he was not even a priest. But he knew something about the church that was more important to Henry than its theology; he knew where its wealth was. It was Cromwell who had dissolved a number of monasteries to raise money for Wolsey's colleges.

At the beginning of 1535, Cromwell's agents combed England, visiting the monasteries and estimating their considerable wealth. What they discovered titillated Henry's avarice so greatly that in the middle of the year a new set of commissioners was sent out to find evidence that the monastic orders were corrupt and should be suppressed. When the last session of the Reformation Parliament met at the beginning of 1536, it passed an act dissolving the smaller monasteries and seizing their lands and wealth for the crown.

Useless, wasted monasteries had been suppressed both in Henry's time and earlier, in England and on the continent. Often the land and income had been given to education or some other good purpose. But good works were not what Henry or Cromwell had in mind. Cromwell had boasted he would make Henry "the richest king that ever was in England." He would do it with the wealth of the monasteries.

The dissolution of the monasteries began in the summer of 1536. At the same time Henry issued his first religious directive as supreme head. Since the break with Rome, some of his subjects had made the error of thinking they were as free as Henry to form their own religious views. All sorts of heresies had arisen, and the supreme head felt the time had come to explain to his flock just what they could and could not believe.

The Ten Articles he issued were a compromise between the old religion and the new Protestant thought. While not revolutionary, they owed just enough to Luther to frighten the traditionalists, who included most of the common people. Many Englishmen were also disturbed by what was happening to the monasteries. While priors and abbots got sizeable pensions for turning over church property to the government, the monks got little or nothing. Homeless monks wandered about the countryside seeking work in a labor market that was already glutted. Poor people sympathized with them not only because they knew how hunger felt, but because in the past they had often gone to the monasteries for charity.

For not all the monasteries were bad. Many gave alms and food to the poor, sheltered travelers, maintained their religious practices, provided a place of worship for the community, employed the local populace, and educated the young. People were distressed by what was happening to the monasteries, to the religion, to the life they had known. The old days may not have been good, but the new ones did not promise to be better. Bewildered, resentful, frightened, and angry, some of the English rose in rebellion.

The outbreak began in Lincolnshire, in northern England. All during the summer of 1536, the air was thick with rumors. It was said that the king would put a heavy tax on weddings, burials, and christenings, and on white bread, pigs, and geese. It was said that the government was going to seize all the church silver and jewels. It was said that all the churches would be torn down, leaving only one for every five miles.

One of Cromwell's commissioners was to visit the town of Louth on October 1. Fearing their precious church jewels and crosses would be taken from them, an armed mob removed the valuables from the church before he came, not to despoil them but to guard them from Henry's greed. The resentment was contagious, and the movement against the crown flared rapidly through the surrounding countryside.

On October 2 the rebels of Lincolnshire drew up a petition for the king. It protested the dissolution of the monasteries and the new church taxes, and demanded that Henry get rid of Cromwell because he was lowborn, and Cranmer because he was a heretic. The feeling of discontent was so strong that within a few days there were some forty thousand men in arms in Lincolnshire. But they had no leader, and none of the nobles in the area would join their cause, so they contented themselves with sending their petition to the king and waiting.

Henry did not like to be told what to do by his subjects. "How presumptuous are ye," he wrote the rebels, "to find fault with your prince . . . and to take upon you, contrary to God's law and man's law, to rule your prince. . . ." He ordered the duke of Suffolk to prepare an army and vowed "the utter destruction of [the rebels], their wives, and children." Suffolk was ordered to hang as many as possible "for a terrible example of like offenders." Suffolk executed forty-six persons, and the rising in Lincolnshire was crushed within two weeks.

Rebellion had no sooner been extinguished in Lincolnshire when it flamed further north in Yorkshire. Known as the Pilgrimage of Grace, it was primarily a religious uprising. The rebels called themselves pilgrims and wore on their sleeves an emblem with the five wounds of Christ.

The rising in York was far more of a threat to Henry than the earlier one because it was supported by the local nobility. During his reign Henry had continued his father's work of strengthening the central government at the expense of the provincial warlords. The new kind of remote authority emanating from London disturbed both noble and peasant. So did the religious changes, the despoliation of the monasteries, and the heavy new taxes.

The actual leader of the Pilgrimage of Grace, however, was

neither peasant nor noble. He was a highly respected lawyer named Robert Aske. Aske organized not only the commoners but the private armies of the lords who joined the rebellion, and by the end of October, he commanded thirty thousand men.

Henry did not see the pilgrims as subjects with grievances, but as "false traitors and rebels" who had sinned against God and man by rising up not only against their anointed king but against the supreme head of the church. Since he had no standing army, he sent the duke of Norfolk north with some eight thousand men to try to gain time. Norfolk conferred with Aske on October 27. It was agreed that two pilgrims could go to London to speak to the king, and there would be an armistice until he replied.

While the king was extending a deaf ear to the emissaries, he was trying to get Aske assassinated. Failing in this, he sent the emissaries back with some vague promises that all would be well. But the pilgrims did not disperse. On December 6 they presented Norfolk with a comprehensive petition. Among many other things, they wanted papal authority restored in England, the dissolution of the monasteries halted, the religious changes annulled, and Mary legitimatized. They also asked for a pardon for all the rebels and requested that a Parliament be summoned in the north to right their grievances.

Norfolk promised both the pardon and the Parliament. He said the king himself would come to York to deal with their complaints. At this, Aske removed his pilgrim's emblem and said, "We will wear no badge or sign but the badge of our sovereign lord," meaning Henry. He dispersed his army and went to London to confer with the king personally.

Aske's followers were not as trusting. When they saw that

the king's men were bringing cannon and ammunition north, that the pardon had not been issued, that the king did not come, and that no Parliament had been summoned, they rightly suspected they had been betrayed, and they rose again. By this time Aske was back in the north, and he wrote to the king begging him to keep his promises. At the same time he begged the people to trust their king.

At this moment the king he so trusted was sending Norfolk very precise orders. "You shall," he said, "cause such dreadful execution to be done upon a good number of every town, village, and hamlet that have offended in this rebellion, as well by the hanging them up in trees, as by the quartering them, and the setting up of their heads and quarters in every town, great and small, and in all such other places, as they may be a fearful spectacle to all others hereafter that would practice in any like manner."

Henry was especially eager that monks be punished, since he mistakenly believed they had incited the rebellion. He specifically ordered the abbot and monks who had returned to a certain suppressed monastery be hanged from the steeple. Altogether, Henry had about two hundred and fifty persons executed for the Yorkshire rising, including Robert Aske.

The Pilgrimage of Grace was the most serious rebellion Henry faced in his long reign. Henry's father had toppled Richard III with a far smaller army and much less support. At the time of the pilgrimage, Henry was so hated and Aske had so strong an army that had he marched south he might well have been able to halt the Reformation in England and put Mary on the throne. But Aske was no challenger for Henry. Henry was a man of blood who understood force, not reason. Aske trusted his king, but his king trusted no one. "Three may keep counsel if two are away, and if I thought my cap knew my counsel, I would throw it into the fire," he once said.

Henry was saved not only by Aske's innocence but also by circumstances no one in England could control. Neither Charles nor Francis could take advantage of the rebellion, as they might otherwise have done, since they were again at war with each other. Rather than meddling in Henry's domestic problems, both were seeking his alliance.

Pope Paul III, however, did try to profit by the insurrection. He sent an English noble, Reginald Pole, to the Netherlands to try to raise a force to invade England. But Pole, a Yorkist claimant to the throne, did not set out on his mission until the rebellion was nearly over. He did not have enough money to hire mercenaries and he could get no support from either Charles or Francis. Henry tried to have Pole murdered, and he barely managed to return to Rome alive.

By the summer of 1537, the threat to Henry's rule had evaporated and his third queen, Jane Seymour, was pregnant. On October 12 she gave birth to a son. The boy was christened Edward, after Henry's Yorkist grandfather.

Ten years after he had set out to rid himself of Catherine and sire a male heir to the throne, Henry had finally succeeded. But Jane Seymour did not share his triumph. Twelve days after making her contribution to king and country, she died. Henry ordered a magnificent funeral for her and, while she was still lying in state, told Cromwell to find him another wife.

While Cromwell was playing Cupid for Henry, he was continuing the enriching task of dissolving the monasteries. The original act of 1536 had called for the suppression of only the smaller houses, but the failure of the Pilgrimage of Grace convinced Cromwell that the larger ones could be taken as well. Within four years virtually all of the nine hundred monasteries, nunneries, and friaries in England and Wales had been dissolved. Once the deed was done, the right to do it was confirmed in a new act passed by Parliament in 1539.

Some abbots attempted defiance, but torture, hanging, and quartering made them and others more compliant. Some attempted bribes; the money was pocketed and the monasteries dissolved anyway. Some were more than willing to surrender their sacred property in return for large government pensions.

By the sixteenth century the monasteries may have become relics of a dying age, but they had once been the focus of religious dedication. There had been a time when all that was beautiful and valuable was given to God. The monasteries were among the most magnificent buildings in Europe and they held priceless and irreplaceable treasures of religious art and craftsmanship.

The men who dissolved the monasteries saw not the beauty but the gold. Henry's commissioners, the local people, and sometimes the monks themselves joined in trying to cart off all the portable wealth before it could be shipped to London. Even Cromwell had a private cache of stolen church jewels.

Men stripped the lead from the roofs of the buildings, broke away the carvings, and destroyed the magnificent paintings and frescoes. The decimated structures shriveled into ruin or were dismantled so that the building materials could be used for fortifications. Religious objects of every sort, the masterpieces of long-dead craftsmen, were melted down for the value of their metal. Vestments were ripped apart for their golden thread. Hand-lettered volumes which recorded the thought and learning of the Middle Ages were torn up and scattered to the winds. Illuminated pages were used to wipe boots and polish candlesticks.

Not only were the monasteries destroyed, but also the shrines, where bodies and relics of saints were revered. One of the richest and most important shrines in Christendom was the tomb of St. Thomas Becket at Canterbury. Pilgrims came there from all over Europe to gape or to pray.

Becket had been dead over three hundred and fifty years, but Henry regarded him as a personal enemy since he had died in defense of the rights of the church. Becket's shrine was plundered and its valuables were toted to London in twenty-six wagonloads. The handsomest jewel on the tomb was made into a ring for Henry's thumb. Becket's bones were burned to ashes, and the ashes were fired from a cannon so that no trace of the saint remained. No one who defied him, even symbolically, could ever be dead enough for Henry.

Once the monasteries were seized, the monks driven off, and the shrines stripped, all became the property of the king of England. What would he do with this incalculable treasure? He promised he would found universities for scholars, schools for the poor, hospitals for the sick. But when the wealth was in his hands, Henry forgot most of his promises. Some of the riches were needed to cover the expenses of his extravagant court. Some were distributed to Henry's friends or advisers, men like Norfolk, Suffolk, and Cromwell. The vast monastic estates and much that was on them were given or sold to the nobles and the upper middle class to win them over to the religious revolution. What was left was used to pay the costs of Henry's next war.

If the suppression of the monasteries had been done in the spirit of reform, what was good and valuable would have been preserved, and their wealth, given to education and other good causes, would have made England the most enlightened country in the world. But the dissolution was done to show that Henry was indeed master of the church, to fill the king's purse and expand his power, and to win the support of the nobles and landowners.

Henry succeeded only partially. His power was expanded and the wealthy did accept the bribe, so that the possibility of a counter-reformation was eliminated. But Henry's leaky purse would not stay filled. Some ten years from the time the dissolution of the monasteries began, the richest king in Christendom was to die deeply in debt.

# 11 ☙ More Wives, More Wars

THE FINAL decade of Henry's life was cluttered, but it was all a reprise of the earlier years. There were more wives, more wars, more executions, devious diplomacy with first one nation then another, and the wavering between Catholic and Protestant that ended in being neither.

Henry remained a bachelor for two years after Jane Seymour's death in October, 1537, not because he wanted to but because he was trying to arrange the most advantageous diplomatic match. Jane died so soon that Henry had not had enough time to fall in love with someone else at court, so he was agreeable to a foreign bride. Besides, he feared that when Francis and Charles got around to halting their latest war, either one or both might turn on him.

To guard against this, Henry worked out all sorts of marriage combinations, for himself and his three children, first with one side, then the other. Henry was fussy about his choice, both diplomatically and personally. At one point he asked Francis to send all of the Frenchwomen he was considering to Calais, so he could inspect them. "The thing touches me too near," he complained. "I wish to see them and know them some time before deciding." But Francis refused, with a sharp retort about "trotting out the young ladies like geldings."

Henry also made life more difficult for potential matchmakers by shifting his standards. At one point he said he was a big man and needed a big wife. Later he was smitten by the dimpled, sixteen-year-old daughter of the former king of Denmark. The girl, who had been married at thirteen and widowed at fourteen, is supposed to have said that if she had two heads she would be happy to put one at Henry's disposal.

While Henry was seeking his fourth wife, Charles and Francis confirmed his worst fears by signing a ten-year truce in the summer of 1538. Pope Paul III decided to take advantage of the unaccustomed lull by calling on the Catholic princes to punish Henry. He was particularly incensed, as was much of Europe, by word which came from England of the plunder of the monasteries and shrines. The pope asked James V of Scotland to invade from the north and sent Reginald Pole to speak to Charles and Francis about joint action against the schismatic king.

Menaced by the possibility of a triple invasion, England united behind Henry in panic and patriotism. The king personally journeyed to the coasts to order the defenses strengthened. Barricades were built of stones carted from the monasteries, ditches were dug, the fleet was made ready, and troops were mustered. To be certain that invaders were not assisted by English treason, Henry beheaded Reginald Pole's older brother, as well as two other Yorkist nobles, and Pole's aged mother was thrown into the Tower.

Pole's mission, which cost him his family, was unsuccessful.

Francis was not anxious to invade England unless Charles did, and Charles was not very anxious at all. The merchants in the Netherlands were just as unwilling to halt the profitable English trade as the merchants in England. Besides, the Turks were threatening Charles's possessions as they thrust into central Europe.

But Henry could not be sure what Charles might do, so he looked for allies among the Protestant princes of Germany. Although Henry was no longer Roman Catholic, he was not quite Protestant either. For many months German and English envoys worked at achieving a theological and political union. Theologically they made little progress, for Henry kept weaving back and forth between the orthodox and the revised in religious styles, depending on which side he wished to placate.

The Ten Articles he had issued in 1536 upheld only three of the seven sacraments and tried to suppress the superstitious worship of images. In 1537 he had taken a step back toward Catholicism when the *Institution of a Christian Man* or *Bishops' Book* was issued, upholding more orthodox views and mentioning all of the sacraments, including the four that had been dropped. But that same year Henry gave permission for the Bible to be published in English and to have certain prayers read to every congregation in English; these were major reforms.

In 1539 Henry took another step back to orthodoxy when Parliament passed the Act of Six Articles, which provided fines, prison, and death for those who did not support traditional doctrine on such matters as clerical celibacy, confession, and private masses. Like most of Henry's theological moves, it was self-serving. Its purpose was to reassure his own people and the Catholic powers abroad that he was basically orthodox at a time when the pope was trying to punish him for being otherwise.

Although England would not compromise with the Protestant envoys theologically, Thomas Cromwell suggested sealing a diplomatic match by marrying Europe's most eligible bachelor to a German princess. Negotiations were begun with the duke of Cleves, whose territory lay northeast of the Netherlands and would be handy for an invasion of Charles's domains if ever the emperor proved to be too prickly. The duke of Cleves was, like Henry, neither Catholic nor Protestant, but somewhere in between, and he had two unmarried sisters.

Henry sent the painter, Hans Holbein the Younger, to Cleves to paint portraits of the two women. From the portraits he chose Anne, the elder of the two, who was twenty-four. The marriage treaty was signed in October, 1539, and Anne was shipped off to England. The impatient forty-nine-year-old bridegroom galloped off to greet her and immediately regretted his haste.

"I like her not," he said bluntly and called her "a great Flanders mare." He asked Cromwell, who had made the match for him, if there was any way he could unmake it. There wasn't. If Henry repudiated Anne so crudely he would alienate the duke of Cleves, as well as the other German princes, and this he dared not do, especially since Charles and Francis were meeting in Paris at that very time.

"Is there none other remedy," he asked his advisers piteously, "but that I must needs, against my will, put my neck in the yoke?" As he prepared for his wedding on January 6, 1540, he muttered to Cromwell, "My lord, if it were not to satisfy the world and my realm, I would not do that I must do this day for none earthly thing."

Henry found Anne of Cleves so repulsive that he never consummated his fourth marriage. Portraits show that she was no uglier than any of his other wives, so the problem may have been one of personality. Henry's first wife was intelligent, his second was vivacious, his third was gentle. Anne of Cleves was simply dull. She spoke only her own language, which was unfamiliar to Henry; she was uneducated; and she could neither sing nor play an instrument; all she could do was sew. She was not the kind of woman to bring either cheer or comfort to an aging king.

Henry had the marriage annulled as soon as it was politic for him to do so. In July, 1540, Convocation found the marriage null and void, and Parliament confirmed this judgment. Anne was just as happy to be rid of Henry as he was to be rid of her. She was given two manors and a large pension, and she chose to remain in England. "As to her who is now called Madame de Cleves," wrote the French ambassador, "far from pretending to be married, she is as joyous as ever, and wears new dresses every day."

Neither Henry nor Anne suffered from the aborted marriage, but the king was angry enough about the mismatch to let his wrath fall somewhere. During the spring of 1540, two factions struggled for power at court. One was led by Cromwell, who was the king's chief adviser, even though Sir Thomas Audley held the title of lord chancellor. This party was responsible for the religious changes, the German alliance, and the disastrous marriage. There was another faction led by the duke of Norfolk and Stephen Gardiner,

Wolsey's former secretary, who had risen to power. This group opposed the German alliance and favored both the old religion and keeping the king's business out of the hands of upstarts like Cromwell.

After taking one look at Anne of Cleves, Henry was willing to call the German policy a failure. He began to listen to Norfolk's view, particularly since the duke baited his argument with another one of his nieces, Catherine Howard, a short, plump, empty-headed, and cheerful nineteen-year-old, who served as a lady-in-waiting to Anne of Cleves.

As Cromwell entered the palace on June 10, a gust of wind blew off his bonnet. Custom and courtesy demanded that the other members of the king's council remove their hats immediately, but none did. "A high wind, indeed," said Cromwell sarcastically, "to blow my bonnet off and keep all yours on."

The other members of the council went to their chamber without him. When he joined them he said, "You were in a great hurry, gentlemen, to begin." Then Norfolk cried out, "Cromwell, do not sit there. Traitors do not sit with gentlemen!"

At this signal, the door opened and the captain of the guard came in with six men to arrest him. Cromwell rose, threw his bonnet to the floor, and cried, "This is the reward for my services! On your consciences, am I a traitor?"

Cromwell was taken to the Tower and accused of heresy and treason. The man who sent so many others to death less deserved than his wrote Henry an abject letter in which he cried for "mercy, mercy, mercy." But the king was too besotted with his pretty new toy to listen. Cromwell was beheaded on July 28, and Henry chose that very day to make Catherine Howard his fifth bride. Among the gifts he gave her were the estates he had confiscated from the fallen Cromwell.

For most of his reign, Henry had been dependent on two great ministers, Wolsey and Cromwell. With Cromwell's death the chief executive finally became Henry himself and the king's business was administered by an inner ring of councillors who came to be called the privy council.

If Henry had a plan in the last years of his life, it was to renew his dream of conquering France. Many years earlier, in 1519, Henry had said, "We wish all potentates to content themselves with their own territories; we are satisfied with this island of ours." But Henry was never satisfied with his island; all his life he lusted after France more than he lusted after any woman.

Before he could return to his overseas adventures, however, Henry had to tidy up his relations with his subjects and neighbors. In 1536 the union of England and Wales had been completed. In 1541 the Irish Parliament decided that Henry should be called king rather than lord of Ireland.

But all was not peace and love within Henry's domains. Early in 1541 there was another uprising in the north. The news came at a time when Henry was both ill and depressed. For years he had suffered from an ulcer on his thigh, probably caused by varicose veins, as well as severe headaches which dated back to 1524, when he had been struck in the head by a spear while jousting. As the years passed, Henry's appetite for sport had diminished, but not his appetite for food. From 1514 to 1541 his waist swelled from thirty-five to fifty-four inches and the French ambassador described him as "very stout and marvellously excessive in eating and drinking."

In time both legs became ulcerated and gave way beneath his crushing weight. Confined to bed with pain and fever, he reacted to the news of the northern rebellion by tossing people into the Tower and executing some who were already there, including Reginald Pole's seventy-year-old mother.

But Henry recovered both his health and his good spirits, and in the summer he went on a progress, or royal tour, of the north. He hoped to pacify the area, where there had been so much riot and rebellion, and he wanted to meet his nephew, King James V of Scotland, to settle their differences so that James would not invade when Henry went back to war with France.

The royal progress had plenty of pomp and elegance to dazzle the northerners and plenty of soldiers and arms to discourage further thoughts of rebellion. Henry was well received wherever he went, and he jovially pardoned those who had rebelled five years earlier. It was a triumphant journey, but it ended badly. Henry waited at York for the king of Scotland but James never came.

Worse things were to happen when Henry returned home. On November 2 Archbishop Thomas Cranmer timidly presented the king with written evidence that his fifth wife, Catherine Howard, had been generous with her affections before her marriage. Henry loved Catherine, or at least he found her a comfort in his old age. At first he denounced the charges as lies, since he didn't want to lose her. But further investigation revealed that Catherine not only had lovers before her marriage but afterward as well.

At this Henry went wild with rage. He called for a sword to

*137*

kill Catherine, saying, "She never had such delight in her lovers as she shall have torture in her death!" When he was calmer he sobbed and complained of his bad luck in choosing wives.

Henry did not have to kill Catherine himself; he had the machinery of the state to settle his domestic quarrels for him. The queen was beheaded on February 13, 1542, and buried not far from the body of her cousin, Anne Boleyn.

Henry was a widower again, but for the moment he did not seek another wife. He turned from Cupid to Mars. In 1541 he had decided to ally himself with Charles once more in order to conquer France. King and emperor agreed to a joint invasion in 1543. To pass the time while waiting for the main event, Charles and Francis resumed their perpetual war in 1542.

Before he could be ready for his invasion of France, Henry had to settle with Scotland, or the Scots would attack while his armies were abroad. In October, 1542, Henry sent Norfolk on a punitive mission across the Scottish border. The following month the English defeated a large Scottish army at Solway Moss. A few weeks later King James V, murmuring, "All is lost!" died of fever and grief, leaving as his sole heir an infant daughter, Mary.

With the Scottish king dead, Henry tried to consolidate his position politically rather than by war because he was saving his firepower for Francis. His plan was to wed Mary, queen of Scots, to his son Edward and unite the two kingdoms. This would mean Scotland would have to break with Rome and France, which the Scottish nobles were not willing to do. But to gain time they signed a peace treaty with England on July 1, 1543, and betrothed Mary to Edward.

Less than two weeks later, on July 12, Henry married his sixth wife, the third named Catherine. She was Catherine Parr, a thirty-one-year-old gentlewoman who had been widowed twice. Although she leaned to the Protestant, she was much like Henry's first Catherine. She was well learned, a patron of the humanists, and a kind woman. For the first time in their lives, Henry's three children lived together with each other and with their father and stepmother. Catherine Parr had no special politics to push, no grudges to bear, no axes to grind, no work for the headsman. In marrying her, Henry got a better bargain than she did. Anne of Cleves remarked tartly, "A fine burden Madame Catherine hath taken on herself."

Although Catherine Parr was a moderate Protestant, she did not influence Henry's theology, which continued to whirl in circles. The struggle continued between the traditionalists, like Norfolk, and the revisionists, like Cranmer. The year Henry married for the last time, he issued his last religious pronouncement, *A Necessary Doctrine and Erudition for Any Christian Man,* commonly called *The King's Book. The King's Book* came down so hard on the side of the orthodox that Chapuys, Charles's ambassador, reported that Henry had restored everything in the old religion except the pope's authority.

However, when the Catholics decided they were strong enough to get rid of Cranmer, they failed. Henry was told that the archbishop was a heretic. He listened carefully and agreed that Cranmer should be arrested at the council table, like Cromwell. But that night he summoned Cranmer and warned him of the plot. He gave Cranmer a ring and told him that when he was arrested, he should show it and ask to be heard by the king himself.

The masque was played as Henry wrote it. Cranmer was seized at the council table and, like the hero of a fairy tale, he produced the magic ring and spoke the magic incantation. "By this token," said the archbishop, "[the king] resumes the matter into his own hand." The councillors knew they had been foiled. When they came before the king, he praised Cranmer and ordered them to "use not my friends so."

But when it served his purposes, Henry could still persecute both sides with impartial cruelty. Two days after Cromwell was beheaded for heresy and treason, Henry hanged three Catholic priests and burned three Protestant heretics. The French ambassador wrote that, "It was wonderful to see adherents to the two opposing parties dying at the same time, and it gave offense to both." He added that both sides protested the perversion of justice "in that they had never been called to judgment, nor knew why they were condemned. . . ." Another observer commented, "People did not inquire much, as it is no new thing to see men hanged, quartered, or beheaded, for one thing or another, sometimes for trifling expressions construed as against the king."

Henry had hoped to invade France in the summer of 1543, but the Scottish negotiations had delayed all action until the fighting season was almost over, so that major engagements had to be postponed until 1544. But before Henry could sink his teeth into France, Scotland nipped his ankle again. In December, 1543, the pro-French, pro-church party, led by the French mother of the infant queen, annulled the treaties with Henry and renewed the French alliance.

Henry ordered an army led by Lord Hertford, Jane Seymour's brother and uncle to the future king, to Scotland in the spring of 1544 to burn, sack, and murder in "as many towns and villages about Edinburgh as you may conveniently." For the moment Henry could not afford a larger war with Scotland because the French war was imminent.

With the last surge of an aging warrior who had always hidden behind the lines, Henry planned to lead his army to France himself. This plan frightened his allies far more than it did his enemies. Henry was now fifty-three years old, bloated to the point of caricature, crippled by failing legs, and often ill. Both his privy council and Charles feared he would be more of a burden to the army than an inspiration. They offered him tactful reasons why he should not go, but he brushed them aside. He arrived in Calais in mid-July to lead his last campaign.

When he got there, the campaign was in a muddle, for no one could agree on strategy. Charles wanted to march on Paris, but Henry decided to settle down for a siege of the city of Boulogne. He enjoyed it immensely, as he had always enjoyed playing at war. He wrote his wife how busy he was, "caring for everything ourself."

Boulogne fell to the English on September 18, and, after claiming it in person, Henry returned to England, leaving Norfolk and Suffolk in command. This was not a war the French wanted and for weeks they had been trying to make peace with either or both of their enemies. Henry had put them off because he had his heart set on Boulogne. But the day he rode into the city in triumph, Charles agreed to make peace with Francis. He also offered to act as mediator between the kings of England and France, but Henry refused to make peace. The French wanted Boulogne back, and Henry would not give it up. So the war went on.

By the following spring, Henry was in serious trouble, for the French were threatening to invade England. Henry cast about desperately for an ally, but neither Charles nor the German princes would have him. His gluttonous war policy had succeeded in isolating England. It had also succeeded in bankrupting her.

The wealth of the monasteries was not enough to pay for Henry's war, nor was the income of the church, which now flowed into Henry's coffers. Henry extorted forced gifts and loans from his squirming subjects, but that wasn't enough either, so the king debased the country's gold and silver coins by using more and more cheap metal. Even this was not enough for Henry, so he dissolved colleges and chapels of priests who did not belong to regular orders.

In the summer of 1545, England faced invasion in a war that no one but Henry wanted, and which he could have concluded at any time by returning Boulogne. One thing Henry had done for his island country was build a strong navy, and now some one hundred ships with twelve thousand men waited for the French.

Henry was dining aboard his flagship, the *Great Harry*, when the French fleet was sighted on July 19. He quickly went ashore, but he need not have bothered. Although they had twice as many ships as the English, the French stayed only long enough to make a few quick shore sorties, then they withdrew.

By the end of the year, the European situation was more confused than threatening. Even Henry's councillors thought the war was costly and pointless. "Our war is noisome to our realm," wrote

Stephen Gardiner. "We are in a world where reason and learning prevail not, and covenants are little regarded. . . ."

The king's council wanted to give Boulogne back in order to have peace, but Henry clung to it. In the manner of princes everywhere and at all times, Henry assured his people he was waging his war in France, "not for our pleasure, but for your defense."

Henry wanted Charles on his side again, but the emperor had turned to battle the German Protestants. The German Protestants were eager for peace between England and France because they wanted both nations to help them battle the emperor. On the other hand Charles wanted both Henry and Francis to help him hammer the Protestants. And everyone suspected that everyone else would betray him at the earliest opportunity, which was probably true.

Early in 1546 Henry made plans for another invasion of France in the spring. But before the war could be resumed, Henry decided to make peace after all, although he insisted he would not surrender Boulogne, "which we have royally conquered in our just wars." "When princes conspire to oppress and exhaust a commonwealth, they call it a 'just war,' " Erasmus had once said. After much bickering a peace treaty was signed on June 7. England agreed not to make war on Scotland unless the Scots attacked first. Henry could keep Boulogne for eight years, after which France could have it back for a fortune in ransom.

In spite of this treaty, Henry was not really at peace. He spent the last months of his life preparing for another attack on Scotland and negotiating now for an alliance with Charles against the French, now for an alliance with the French and Germans against Charles.

Henry's final months were just as muddled at home as they

were abroad. The country was divided between Catholics and Protestants, with various shadings in between. For this the supreme head of the church, in his last speech to Parliament on Christmas eve, 1545, blamed the clergy, who "preach one against another, teach one contrary to another . . . without charity or discretion."

Henry also reprimanded laymen for discussing and examining the Scriptures, when their true interpretation was his function, committed to him "by God." "I am very sorry to know and hear," he said, "how unreverently that most precious jewel, the word of God, is disputed, rhymed, sung, and jangled in every alehouse and tavern. . . ."

However, Henry was, on the whole, satisfied with his people. "No prince in the world more favoreth his subjects than I do you," he said, "nor no subjects or commons more love and obey their sovereign lord than I perceive you do me. . . ."

If there was religious confusion and discord in England, it came from the supreme head himself. He broke with Rome but demanded that his revisions become the new orthodoxy. Even if his people were willing to stand behind him, they would have difficulty knowing which way he faced. While Catholics and Protestants struggled for power, Henry swung his considerable bulk first one way, then the other, depending on whether he was negotiating with or against Charles. The first half of 1546 saw a period of witch hunts directed against the Protestants and led by Stephen Gardiner and Thomas Wriothesley, the new lord chancellor. One of the victims was very nearly the queen herself.

Being a learned woman, Catherine Parr often discussed religious matters with Henry. Once, after she left his chamber, Henry remarked bitterly to Gardiner, "A good hearing it is, when women become such clerks; and a thing much to my comfort, to come in mine old days to be taught by my wife."

Since Gardiner opposed Catherine's Protestantism, he took advantage of Henry's anger to say that the council could prove she was a treasonous heretic. Henry agreed to have her investigated, and when the articles of accusation were drawn up, he signed them.

Word of the plot carried to Catherine, who knew how to save her head. She went directly to Henry to beg his pardon and assure him that she submitted to his superior wisdom. She would not presume to instruct anyone as learned as he and she would forever be obedient to him in all things. She had only discussed theology with him in order to get his mind off the pain in his legs.

Henry approved of humility in others. "And is it even so, sweetheart, and tended your argument to no worse end?" he asked. "Then perfect friends we are now again as ever at any time heretofore."

The next day the forgetful king was strolling with Catherine and three other ladies who were to be arrested with her, when the lord chancellor, who did not know about the reconciliation, came to take them to the Tower. The self-righteous king drove off the unlucky minister with cries of "Knave! Arrant knave! Beast! Fool!" Thus Catherine lived to survive Henry and wed again after his death. But others were not so fortunate, and several prominent Protestants were burned alive for heresy.

By midyear, however, the clerical climate had changed. A weather-vane theologian, Henry was turning to the Protestant wind again and speaking of eliminating the mass. The council of regency he appointed to govern the country while his son Edward was a minor was dominated by Protestants, and Edward's tutors were also Protestant.

As far as Henry was concerned, even more important than assuring a Protestant succession was assuring the succession itself. He had not moved heaven and earth to sire a legitimate male heir in order to have the throne pass to someone else. In December, 1546, the duke of Norfolk and his son, the poet Surrey, were sent to the Tower. Surrey, talking too loosely, had suggested his father should rule for Prince Edward.

Surrey was beheaded in January, 1547. His father's execution was scheduled for the morning of January 28, but it was not carried out because Henry VIII died first.

Henry had been ill for months. His ulcerated legs, which had tormented him for many years, grew steadily worse, and because of the pain and his weight, he had to be carried about in a chair. He also suffered from a recurring fever, probably malaria. By December of 1546 he was so clearly dying that he revised his will. It provided that the crown would pass to his nine-year-old son Edward. If Edward died without heirs, he would be succeeded by Mary, the daughter of Catherine of Aragon. If Mary died without heirs, she would be succeeded by Elizabeth, the daughter of Anne Boleyn. If Elizabeth died without heirs, the throne would pass to the descendants of Henry's sister Mary and her second husband, the duke of Suffolk.

By January 27 Henry was sinking rapidly, but no one dared tell him because it was treason to prophesy the death of the king. Finally, the chief gentleman of his chamber, Sir Anthony Denny, had the courage to tell Henry to prepare himself. The king accepted the news calmly and said that although he had sinned, "yet is the mercy of Christ able to pardon me all my sins, though they were greater than they be."

Denny asked Henry if he wanted to see anyone, and Henry asked for Cranmer. But first he wanted to "take a little sleep; and then, as I feel myself, I will advise upon the matter."

Henry slept for a while. When he woke, he sent for Cranmer. By the time the archbishop arrived, Henry could no longer speak. Cranmer asked Henry to give some sign that he trusted in Christ. Henry took Cranmer's hand and wrung it as hard as he could. The king died at about two A.M. on Friday, January 28, 1547.

# EPILOGUE ⌇ *A Spot of Blood and Grease*

JUDGMENTS of Henry VIII range from the brutal to the beatific. Charles Dickens called him "a most intolerable ruffian, a disgrace to human nature, and a spot of blood and grease upon the history of England." The poet Thomas Gray described him as "The majestic lord / that broke the bonds of Rome." To historian A. F. Pollard, author of the standard biography of Henry, he was "the most remarkable man who ever sat on the English throne."

Perhaps it was Cardinal Wolsey, who knew him so well, who offered the greatest insight. "He is a prince of royal courage," said Wolsey, "and he hath a princely heart; and rather than he will miss or want part of his appetite he will hazard the loss of one-half of his kingdom."

Henry was all appetite and all ego. Almost everything he did, good or bad, began as a personal whim which he then swelled into a matter of conscience and high principle.

He lived in an age when the state was more important than any individual except for the king, who was the state. Since nothing could be denied the state, nothing could be denied the king. The English accepted his despotism because they knew no other form of government and because they feared that to challenge it would be to return to the anarchy of the Wars of the Roses. They wanted peace at home so they could become prosperous, and Henry faced more opposition when he rifled the purses of his subjects than when he tampered with their consciences.

Henry did much for England by carrying on the work his father began. He unified the country and left it a more cohesive and prouder land than he had inherited. He ended the conflict between church and state and the interference of foreigners in English affairs by transferring the power of the church from Rome to London. He brought Wales and Ireland into line, although he failed utterly in Scotland. But he put down more overmighty lords, executed more pretenders and, under Wolsey and Cromwell, did more than any of his predecessors to concentrate authority in the central government. He also encouraged a new aristocracy, made up of the middle class on the rise and on the make. In every way he demonstrated how powerful a king could be, but by using Parliament so often to get what he wanted, he strengthened it and increased rather than diminished its role.

But even the good that Henry did was debased by his motives. The humanists believed that reason and knowledge would make better men even of kings, and that a good prince devoted himself to the welfare of his subjects, corrected social injustice, helped the poor and the needy, and educated his people.

Henry believed no such thing. He was not stupid, but he was greedy. His vision extended only as far as his appetites. Unlike his father, who usually tried to do what was good for

England, Henry VIII did what was good for himself, confident that what was good for him must be good for his country.

He brought the Protestant Reformation to England, and whether this is good or bad depends on one's theology. But it was done not out of conviction, but because first he wanted a son and then he wanted Anne Boleyn.

He freed the dying monasteries from the hands of the church, but instead of using the vast wealth for religious reorganization and reform, for education, for the sick, for the poor, he poured it into a war no one remembers. He despoiled the learning and the beauty of the monasteries and used the stones to build fortifications.

He inherited a fortune from his father and spent it all at court. He plundered a larger fortune from the monasteries and spent it all on war. He pocketed the combined income of church and state, yet debased the currency and died in debt.

Most of the humanists who came to court were invited by his wives, not Henry. It was Catherine of Aragon who visited colleges and supported poor scholars while Henry went hunting. The one genius Henry brought to court was Thomas More, and he sent him back without his head. His primary interest in colleges was how much income they could bring him; at the end of his life Henry was considering dissolving the colleges to pay for his wars.

When he built, he built castles and ships, not universities. His ships were for war, not for exploration of the New World, which he left to the other European powers. Since he couldn't see what lay beyond the vast ocean, he didn't want it. Rather than care for the welfare of his people, he beggared them by not taking over the functions of the monasteries.

Henry made England an important diplomatic power by his incessant meddling in European politics, but neither his wars nor his peaces had any lasting effect. Most wars seem pointless to the next generation, but Henry's were pointless even in his own time and to his own contemporaries, since he never could have conquered France.

He freed his nation from Roman domination, but there was more religious freedom before the break than afterward. "A good Catholic," wrote historian Thomas Macaulay, "he preferred to be his own pope." Henry's demand for absolute conformity to the Word as he spoke it created more discord than the nation had known before the schism. The medieval church had allowed so many religious orders, each with its own rules, that there was a wide variety of practice and opinion. Henry's insistence on conformity only splintered the religion into many sects and made for many martyrs.

Since Henry VIII bestrode the world he knew, he thought he would continue to rule it after his death. But all his labors kept his dynasty on the throne for just one more generation. The crown went to Edward, then to Mary, then to Elizabeth. Since none of them had children, it passed from the Tudors forever. It went not to the descendants of his sister Mary, as his will directed, but to the Stuarts, the descendants of his sister Margaret.

Henry VIII was buried in St. George's Chapel at Windsor Castle, next to the body of Jane Seymour, the mother of his heir. But he did not find eternal rest there. It is said that his corpse was burned to ashes at the orders of his daughter Mary when she became queen, a final vengeance for what he had done to her, to her mother, and to her church. His magnificent tomb was stripped and despoiled by order of Parliament during the English Revolution, when Englishmen died for the principle that a king should not govern his people but be governed by them.

# ✍ Selected Bibliography

All of these books are available in paperback editions, and all are exceptionally readable, particularly those by Mattingly and Ferguson.

Bindoff, S. T. *Tudor England*. Middlesex, England: Penguin Books, 1950.

Ferguson, Charles W. *Naked to Mine Enemies; The Life of Cardinal Wolsey*. Boston: Little, Brown, 1958.

Kendall, Paul Murray. *Richard the Third*. Garden City, N. Y.: Doubleday, Anchor Books, 1965.

Mattingly, Garrett. *Catherine of Aragon*. New York: Vintage Books, 1941.

Pollard, A. F. *Henry VIII*. New York: Harper Torchbooks, 1966.

Shakespeare, William. *The Famous History of the Life of King Henry the Eighth*. New York: Signet Classics, 1967.

Trevelyan, G. M. *History of England*. Vols. I, II. Garden City, N. Y.: Doubleday, Anchor Books, 1953.

# ✒ General Bibliography

Bagley, J. J. *Henry VIII.* New York: Arco Publishing, 1963.

Bowle, John. *Henry VIII.* Boston: Little, Brown, 1964.

Chamberlin, Frederick. *The Private Character of Henry the Eighth.* New York: Ives Washburn, 1931.

Elton, G. R. *England Under the Tudors.* London: Methuen, 1955.

Fisher, H. A. L. *The History of England from the Accession of Henry VII to the Death of Henry VIII (1485–1547).* London: Longmans, Green, 1910.

Hackett, Francis. *Henry the Eighth.* New York: Horace Liveright, 1929.

Hall, Edward. *Henry VIII.* London: T. C. & E. C. Jack, 1904.

Luke, Mary M. *Catherine, the Queen.* New York: Coward-McCann, 1967.

Mackie, J. D. *The Earlier Tudors, 1485–1558.* Oxford: Oxford University Press, 1952.

MacNalty, Arthur S. *Henry VIII, A Difficult Patient.* London: Christopher Johnson, 1952.

Morris, Christopher. *The Tudors.* London: B. T. Batsford, 1955.

154

Morrison, N. Brysson. *The Private Life of Henry VIII*. New York: Vanguard Press, 1964.

Mumby, Frank Arthur. *The Youth of Henry VIII*. Boston: Houghton Mifflin, 1913.

Rowse, A. L. *Bosworth Field and the Wars of the Roses*. London: Macmillan, 1966.

Scarisbrick, J. J. *Henry VIII*. Berkeley: University of California Press, 1968.

Smith, H. Maynard. *Henry VIII and the Reformation*. New York: Russell & Russell, 1962.

Temperley, Gladys. *Henry VII*. Boston: Houghton Mifflin, 1914.

Williams, C. H. *England Under the Early Tudors (1485–1529). Illustrated from Contemporary Sources*. London: Longmans, Green, 1925.

Williamson, James A. *The Tudor Age*. New York: David McKay, 1953.

# ✒ Index